Frommer's™

St. Petersburg
day BY day™

1st Edition

by ~~Angela Gilbert~~

Wiley Publishing, Inc.

Contents

UK Publisher: Sally Smith
Executive Project Editor: Daniel Mersey
Commissioning Editor: Mark Henshall
Development Editor: Felicity Caurus
Project Editor: Hannah Clement
Photo Research: Jill Emeny

Wiley also publishes its books in a variety of electronic formats. Some
content that appears in print may not be available in electronic books.

British Library Cataloguing in Publication Data

A catalogue record for this book is available from the British Library

ISBN: 978-0-470-71404-1

Typeset by Wiley Indianapolis Composition Services

Printed and bound in China by RR Donnelley

5 4 3 2 1

A Note from the Editorial Director

Organizing your time. That's what this guide is all about.

Other guides give you long lists of things to see and do and then expect you to fit the pieces together. The Day by Day guides are different. These guides tell you the best of everything, and then they show you how to see it in the smartest, most time-efficient way. Our authors have designed detailed itineraries organized by time, neighborhood, or special interest. And each tour comes with a bulleted map that takes you from stop to stop.

Hoping to lose yourself in the Masterpieces of The Hermitage or see psychedelic domes at the Church of the Spilled Blood? Planning to splash out in the Lobby Bar of the Grand Hotel, where Style Moderne meets New Russian Excess or pay your respects to the city's most famous sons at Nevsky Cemetery?

Whatever your interest or schedule, the Day by Days give you the smartest routes to follow. Not only do we take you to the top attractions, hotels, and restaurants, but we also help you access those special moments that locals get to experience—those "finds" that turn tourists into travelers.

The Day by Days are also your top choice if you're looking for one complete guide for all your travel needs. The best hotels and restaurants for every budget, the greatest shopping values, the wildest nightlife—it's all here.

Why should you trust our judgment? Because our authors personally visit each place they write about. They're an independent lot who say what they think and would never include places they wouldn't recommend to their best friends. They're also open to suggestions from readers. If you'd like to contact them, please send your comments our way at feedback@frommers.com, and we'll pass them on.

Enjoy your Day by Day guide—the most helpful travel companion you can buy. And have the trip of a lifetime.

Warm regards,

Kelly Regan

Kelly Regan, Editorial Director
Frommer's Travel Guides

About the Author

Hillary Gilbert first went to Russia in 1993, for a 5-month language course. She never really went home. Having traveled across Siberia and most countries of the former Soviet Union in the interim, she now splits her time between Moscow and London, running her own editorial services company. Find out more at www.urgentedits.com.

Acknowledgments

I have a great many people to thank for their help in writing this book. They are: David Bamber, Victor and Irina Bereznoi, Peter Brophy, Bartek Cieniawa, Jill Emeny, Mary Anne Evans, Mark Henshall, Nazra Hussain, Melissa Shales. I should also like to thank all of the staff at the Kirov Museum, the Kunstkamera, the Narvskaya Zastava Museum, the Lenin Museum at the Smolny Institute, and the Yelizarov Museum. As ever, I should like to thank Richard Hecquet. Many of the better ideas in this book are, in fact, his.

An Additional Note

Please be advised that travel information is subject to change at any time—and this is especially true of prices. We therefore suggest that you write or call ahead for confirmation when making your travel plans. The authors, editors, and publisher cannot be held responsible for the experiences of readers while traveling. Your safety is important to us, however, so we encourage you to stay alert and be aware of your surroundings.

Star Ratings, Icons & Abbreviations

Every hotel, restaurant, and attraction listing in this guide has been ranked for quality, value, service, amenities, and special features using a **star-rating system.** Hotels, restaurants, attractions, shopping, and nightlife are rated on a scale of zero stars (recommended) to three stars (exceptional). In addition to the star-rating system, we also use a **kids** icon to point out the best bets for families. Within each tour, we recommend cafes, bars, or restaurants where you can take a break. Each of these stops appears in a shaded box marked with a coffee-cup-shaped bullet ☕.

The following **abbreviations** are used for credit cards:

AE American Express	**DISC** Discover	**V** Visa
DC Diners Club	**MC** MasterCard	

Frommers.com

Now that you have this guidebook to help you plan a great trip, visit our web-site at **www.frommers.com** for additional travel information on more than 4,000 destinations. We update features regularly to give you instant access to the most current trip-planning information available. At Frommers.com, you'll find scoops on the best airfares, lodging rates, and car rental bargains. You can even book your travel online through our reliable travel booking partners. Other popular features include:

A Note on Prices

In the "Take a Break" and "Best Bets" sections of this book, we have used a system of dollar signs to show a range of costs for 1 night in a hotel (the price of a double-occupancy room) or the cost of an entrée (main meal) at a restaurant. Use the following table to decipher the dollar signs:

Cost	Hotels	Restaurants
$	under $100	under $10
$$	$100–$200	$10–$20
$$$	$200–$300	$20–$30
$$$$	$300–$400	$30–$40
$$$$$	over $400	over $40

An Invitation to the Reader

In researching this book, we discovered many wonderful places—hotels, restaurants, shops, and more. We're sure you'll find others. Please tell us about them, so we can share the information with your fellow travelers in upcoming editions. If you were disappointed with a recommendation, we'd love to know that, too. Please write to:

Frommer's St. Petersburg, Day by Day, 1st Edition
Wiley Publishing, Inc. • 111 River St. • Hoboken, NJ 07030-5774

22 Favorite
Moments

22 Favorite **Moments**

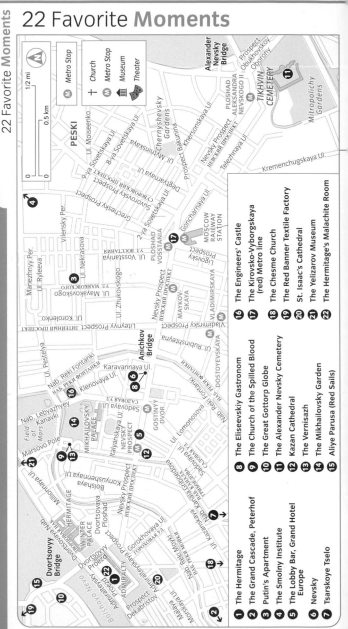

Metro Stop

+ Church
Ⓜ Metro Stop
🏛 Museum
🎭 Theater

1/2 mi
0.5 km

Moscow might have the glitz and the oligarchs, but the real soul of Russia is here, Peter the Great's European capital, scene of the last days of the Romanovs and the Bolshevik Revolution. The most Western of the Russian cities—prosperous until recently and birthplace of Russia's Prime Minister, Vladimir Putin—'Piter' will manage to surprise you from its six-hour mid-winter days to its long and languid White Nights. Be warned though, it's not cheap—particularly in summer, when hotel rates go through the roof. This book will take you through all the must-see sights, and a few not generally known to non-Russian speakers. Without breaking the bank.

❶ The Hermitage. Michelangelo, Leonardo da Vinci, Brueghel, Titian, Rubens, Van Gogh, and Picasso. Don't even hope to do it in one day. *See p 26.*

❷ The Grand Cascade, Peterhof. 72-plus gilded statues, fountains, and thousands of gallons of water a day. All of it driven by gravity alone. *See p 161.*

❸ Putin's Apartment. From a *communalka* (shared apartment) to the Kremlin. *See p 55.*

❹ The Smolny Institute. The heart of the Revolution, and the birthplace of the Great Terror. *See p 41.*

❺ The Lobby Bar, Grand Hotel Europe. Style Moderne architecture meets New Russian excess. Eat *kasha* (porridge) all week for one end-of-holiday budget-busting splurge. *See p 125.*

❻ A night walk along Nevsky. Whatever time of year you go, it's going to rain. Don't fight it. The city is at its best after dark, with the bridges floodlit and the Putin-boom scaffolding hidden from view. *See p 76.*

❼ Tsarskoye Tselo. Much more than Catherine the Great's palace or the Amber Room. Go on the first snowy day of winter to walk across the ice from the Grotto to the Hall on the Island. *See p 156.*

❽ The Eliseevskiy Gastronom. Closed since 2007, but still the city's most outstanding Style Moderne gem. *See p 12.*

❾ The Church of the Spilled Blood. Psychedelic domes and a gruesome history. *See p 8.*

❿ The Great Gottorp Globe. Climbing the five flights to the top of the Kunstkamera will very nearly kill you, but do it anyway. Exquisite artwork illustrating the 17th-century world view. *See p 80.*

⓫ The Alexander Nevsky Cemetery. Pay your respects to the city's most famous sons: Dostoevsky, Tchaikovsky, Mussorgsky, Rimsky-Korsakov, Glinka and others. *See p 53.*

⓬ Watching the sunrise over the Kazan Cathedral. Hung-over and footsore after another White Night. *See p 11.*

The Grand Cascade, Peterhof.

Church of the Spilled Blood.

⑰ The Kirovsko-Vyborgskaya (red) Metro line. Working class heroes at Narvskaya, cut-glass pillars at Avtovo, and the history of the Revolution on bronze plaques at Ploshad Vosstaniya. Stalinist architecture at its most surreal. *See p 23.*

⑱ The Chesme Church. A pink and white candy cane Gothic folly. Directly opposite a former GULAG. *See p 61.*

⑲ The Red Banner Textile Factory. Constructivism at work: a knitwear factory built in the shape of a ship. *See p 60.*

⑳ Panoramic city views from the colonnades of St Isaac's Cathedral. Almost worth risking a heart attack for. *See p 10.*

㉑ The Yelizarov Museum. The discreet charm of the bourgeoisie. As lived by Lenin and his in-laws. *See p 53.*

㉒ ★★★ The Hermitage's Malachite Room. The arrest of the Provincial Government marked the Romanov dynasty's very last day. Historic, beautiful, and some of the best views in the city. *See p 29.* ●

⑬ The Vernisazh. Standard tourist trinkets, but in one of the city's best locations: the Field of Mars on one side, the Church of the Spilled Blood on the other. *See p 15.*

⑭ The Mikhailovsky Garden. Wander down to the river to pick up a boat from Carlo Rossi's Neoclassical pavilion, or spend the day in the lush manicured gardens. Spend the entire day with a book—or a lover. *See p 17.*

⑮ Aliye Parusa (Red Sails). For one night only: tall ships in the Neva, lasers and lightshows on the façades of the Winter Palace, dancing fountains, and gas flares on the Rostral Columns. Why was High School graduation never like this for us? *See p 24.*

⑯ The Engineers' Castle. The madness of Tsar Paul I. *See p 17.*

Yuri Velten's 1780 Chesme Church.

The Best **Full-Day Tours**

PETRO PRIMO
CATHARINA SECUNDA
MDCCLXXXII

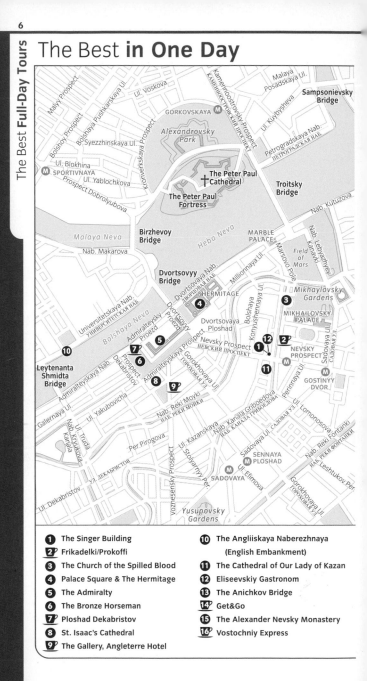

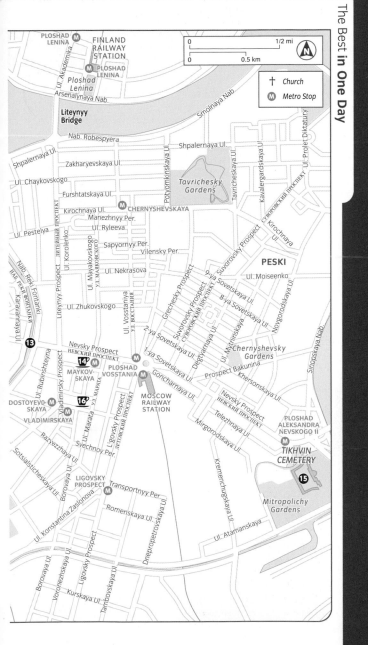

A 'get your bearings' tour taking you from the Winter Palace to the famous dead at the Alexander Nevsky cemetery, via the key sights on main thoroughfare Nevsky Prospect. While the points here have been arranged in a way that makes geographic sense, feel free to mix and match, timing wise: the riverside embankments are a joy to wander as the sun goes down over the Neva. **START: from Nevsky Prospect Metro onto the Griboedov Canal for the Church of the Spilled Blood**

❶ ★★★ The Singer Building.

The first thing you see as you emerge from Nevsky Prospect metro, this classic piece of Style Moderne (p 105) was built for the Singer sewing machine company in 1904. Originally home to the US Embassy, a bank, and a museum of costume—in addition to the Singer offices on the upper floors, busily engaged in supplying uniforms to the Imperial army—it housed Petrogosizdata (the Petrograd State Publishing House), with the Dom Knigi (literally 'House of Books') on the two lower floors. Don't be misled by signs telling you literature is on the second floor: bear right from the entrance for a good selection of novels in English, as well as maps, guidebooks and souvenirs. *Nevsky*

The Style Moderne former Singer building, now Dom Knigi.

Prospect d. 28. ☎ *812 448 2355. 24hr. Metro: Nevsky Prospect.*

❷ ★ Frikadelki/Prokoffi. This is a

long tour, so fill up on traditional Russian salads, coffee and cakes at either of these ultra-cheap buffets on the canal: Frikadelki's best, in my view. *Frikadelki, Nab. Kanala Griboedova d. 8/1.* ☎ *812 571 5135. Prokoffi (same address).* ☎ *314 5629. $.*

❸ ★★★ The Church of the Spilled Blood. Psychedelic domes

on this Russian Revival masterpiece hit you as you turn into the Griboedov Canal. Built in 1883 to commemorate Tsar Alexander II's assassination in 1881 (an ironic end for one of the few Romanov reformers and the liberator of the serfs), this is an orgy of Russian nationalism, built in the nine-domed Muscovy style of St. Basil's cathedral (albeit some 300 years later), with the belfry decorated with the insignia of the cities and regions of Russia, and a series of plaques on the exterior walls celebrating the late 19th century reforms which were to prove their originator's undoing. The canal embankment was extended to allow the church to be built over the exact spot of the assassination, (which is now enshrined), complete with the original cobble stones. With the building only completed in 1907, a decade before the Revolution, the church has never been consecrated and

The Church of the Spilled Blood.

faced repeated threats of demolition throughout the Soviet era, before being made a protected monument in 1968. *Canal Griboedova d. 2a.* ☎ *812 315 1636.* http://eng.cathedral.ru/saviour. *Admission 300R adults, 170R kids. 10am–7pm, closed Wed. Metro: Nevsky Prospect.*

4 ★★★ **Palace Square & The Hermitage.** The main attraction, but impossible to do in one day (or even a week). This timetable allows for two hours or so running through the Hermitage's State Rooms or your personal favorites: Grandmasters, the Italian Renaissance, or the Impressionists. Check the mini-tours on p 26–p 37 and take your pick. The arch through which you'll enter the square was built by Carlo Rossi 1823–1829. Previously the Head Quarters of the General Staff, the left wing is now part of the Hermitage Museum (see p 31). The Alexander Column in the center (August Montferrand, 1832) was erected to commemorate victory over Napoleon in 1812. Named

for Tsar Alexander I (whose face is reproduced on the angel at the top), it took more than 3,000 builders and troops to erect in 1834.

5 ★ **The Admiralty.** Nothing remains of Peter the Great's original fortress and shipyard, built here in 1704, although Konnogvardeisky Bulvar follows the route of the canal which once ran from here to New Holland. The Neoclassical building you see was built by Adrian Zakharov in 1806–1823: it now houses the Naval Engineering Institute, and is closed to the public. Don't miss the ship-shaped weather vane on top of the spire, said to be based on Peter the Great's own korablik or 'little ship'. With the facades facing the river now quite shockingly tatty, this is best viewed from among the statues (and beer tents) of the Alexandrovsky Sad (the Maxim Gorky Workers' Garden until 1989). Directly behind, the building at No. 2 (now the Museum of the History of the Political Police) previously housed Felix Dzerzhinsky's Extraordinary Commission, an early forerunner to the KGB (see p 69). *Admiralteysky Proezd d. 1.*

Carlo Rossi's Admiralty Arch.

Russian Museums: Need to Know

Dual Pricing: Some museums still operate dual pricing for Russian nationals and foreigners: 'foreigner' rates are shown throughout this guide. **Opening Times**: Russian museums close one day a week, usually Monday. Many also close for cleaning (the so-called 'sanitary den') usually—although by no means always—on the final Monday of every month. **Floor Numbering**: What Europeans call the ground floor will be the first floor in Russia. This system is used throughout this book.

6 ★★ **The Bronze Horseman.** Taking its name from Pushkin's well-loved poem of 1833, this monument was commissioned by Catherine the Great in 1782, mounted on the 'Thunder Stone', a 1,600 ton boulder from Konnaya-Lakhta. The somewhat immodest inscription reads: 'To Peter the First. From Catherine the Second.' The square on which it sits was formed when the Senate and Synod (Carlo Rossi, 1834) were built along its western side. Now home to the Constitutional Court, look out for the plaque on the Senate commemorating the December 1825 uprising from which the square takes its name, where army officers led 3,000 troops in protest at Nicholas I's accession to the throne. You'll find some (all too rare) restrooms at the top of Konnogvardeisky Bulvar, between the Synod and the former Imperial Stables (the Manege). *Ploshad Dekabristov.*

7 ★★★ **Ploshad Dekabristov.** Steer clear of the shashlik (kebabs) at this chaotic summer café facing the river, but be sure to stop for a beer: the nightly karaoke is just too hilarious to miss, as the fifty-plus generation belt out classic 1960s party-political pop. *Ploshad Dekabristov. No phone. $.*

8 ★★★ **St. Isaac's Cathedral.** With its colonnades open until 4am during summer, this must be the city's most romantic venue. The third cathedral to stand on this site (Peter the Great was married in the first), this was built by Auguste de Montferrand (together with more than half a million laborers over 40 years) and consecrated in 1858. Personally, I never pay the 300-ruble entrance fee: save your time to drink in the exquisite sculpture on the portico and dome. *Isaakievskaya Ploshad d.1.* ☎ *812 315 9732. http://eng.cathedral.ru. Cathedral tickets 300R adults, 170R kids, colonnade 150R adults, 100R kids, 300R after 7pm.Cathedral 10am–7pm (and 7pm–10.30pm summer), colonnade 10am–6pm (and 7pm–4am summer). Closed Wed.*

9 ★★★ **The Gallery, Angleterre Hotel.** Allegedly the poor relation to the Astoria next door, although I've never understood why. Stop for coffee in its perfectly preserved 1912 Art Deco interior, directly overlooking St Isaac's Square. *M. Morskaya Ul. d. 24.* ☎ *812 494 5125. $$.*

10 The Angliiskaya Naberezhnaya (English Embankment). It's a fascinating walk along Bolshaya Morskaya back to Nevsky

The Cathedral of Our Lady of Kazan.

Prospect if you're so minded, but summer visitors shouldn't pass up the chance to enjoy a drink with the rest of the population at the summer cafes along the river bank. Don't miss the ornate Palace of Weddings at No. 28, or the monument in front of No. 44 (now the Museum of the History of St Petersburg, see p 49), marking the spot at which the *Avrora Cruiser* was moored the night the Revolution started, 25th October 1917.

⓫ **The Cathedral of Our Lady of Kazan.** With the colonnade currently under scaffolding, and with a very relaxed approach to rubble removal, Andrei Voronikhin's Neoclassical masterpiece (built in 1801–1811) isn't looking its best. It's worth a visit just to marvel at any government that could turn a building like this (in 1932) into a 'Museum of the History of Religion and Atheism'. The two statues in front are to Mikhail Kutuzov (hero of the Napoleonic War, buried in the chapel on the left-hand side) and Barclay de Tolly, Minister of War during Napoleon's invasion in 1812. *Kazanskaya Ploshad d. 2.* ☎ *812 318 2548. Admission free. Daily, 8am–8pm. Metro: Nevsky Prospect.*

Telephone Numbers

The 812 St Petersburg city code is shown throughout this guide. If dialing long-distance, you'll need to prefix the number you're calling with '8' and wait for a tone before dialing the number. For international calls, dial '8', wait for a tone, then dial '10' before dialing the country code: see Savvy Traveler, p 163. Many small businesses here use mobile phones: these are 10-digit numbers, always prefixed with '8'.

⑫ ★★★ Eliseevskiy Gastronom. This Style Moderne masterpiece, opened by the Eliseev brothers in 1903 (and the Soviet-era 'Gastronom No. 1'), has been closed since January 2007, no longer viable in the face of Nevsky's soaring rents, and the city government's insistence it remain a grocery. The original fittings are still in place, however, so peer through the doors for a glimpse of the stained glass lining the main hall, and don't miss A.G. Adamson's allegorical sculptures (Industry, Commerce, Art and Science) outside. *Nevsky Prospect d. 28. Metro: Nevsky Prospect.*

Statue at the Eliseevskiy Gastronom.

although others claim it is the face of his worst enemy, or his mistress. Pick up the green line (Line 3) at Gostiny Dvor metro and it's two stops directly to Ploshad Alexandra Nevskovo.

⑭ Get&Go. In a city where it's all too easy to spend $6 on a cup of coffee, it's worth breaking your journey at Mayakovskaya metro for this deli-style coffee bar in the Nevsky Atrium shopping mall. Fresh croissants and American style coffee for less than you'd pay at home. *Nevsky Prospect d. 71. No phone. $.*

⑬ The Anichkov Bridge. Don't get back on the metro without taking a moment to snap the Horse Tamers on each corner of this bridge, the first to be built in St Petersburg, in 1715. Peter Klodt von Urgensburg's statues were erected in 1851, Tsar Nicholas I had sent previous versions to Prussia and Naples. Urban myth has it that the sculptor—out of sheer frustration—carved the Tsar's face in the veins of one of the horses,

⑮ The Alexander Nevsky Monastery. Founded by Peter the Great in 1710 to celebrate Alexander Nevsky's victory over Sweden in 1240, the Tikhvinskoye Cemetery has been the final resting place of St Petersburg's favorite sons since 1823. See p 54 for the full tour, or simply pay your respects to Tchaikovsky, Dostoevsky, Mikhail Glinka, Modest Mussorgsky, Nikolai Rismky-Korsakov,

Horse tamers on the Anichkov Bridge.

The Alexander Nevsky Monastery.

Anton Rubinstein, and the city's perestroika reformist mayor, Anatoly Sobchak. *Ploshad Alexandra Nevskovo d. 1* ☎ *812 274 1113,* ☎ *812 274 2635. www.lavra.spb. ru/. Admission 60R. Daily 9.30am–5.30pm, closed Wed. Metro: Ploshad Alexandra Nevskovo.*

16 ★★★ **Vostochniy Express.** Perfect Russian cooking and cheap prices: one to remember and come back to. Ignore the pricier restaurant next door in favor of the informal 'buffet' offering traditional soups, main courses, and fabulous *hachapuri* (Georgian cheese-filled bread). Feed a family from 350 rubles a head. *Ul. Marata d. 21.* ☎ *812 314 5096. $$.*

St Petersburg by Night

You can pick up a boat almost anywhere in the center but for a midnight cruise head down to the Admiralteisky Quay, right at the water's edge, opposite the *Tsar Carpenter* statue of Peter the Great and guarded by two marble lions, it's impossible to miss. Tickets sell out fast, so get there early and take advantage of the many summer beer tents. Boat tickets are available at Kassa No. 1, Lion Quay, Admiralteiskaya Nab. d. 2. ☎ 812 716 5886, ☎ 812 233 4577. Night trips 450R, 500R weekends. Or try AstraMarine, Admiralteiskaya Nab. d. 2. ☎ 812 320 0877. If you prefer dry land, you'll find numerous night-time bus tours among the bargain coaches to Helsinki outside the Bukvoed bookshop on Ploshad Vosstaniya. Admiral Tours depart at 11pm every night. Ploshad Vosstaniya. ☎ 812 971 5050.

The Best **in Two Days**

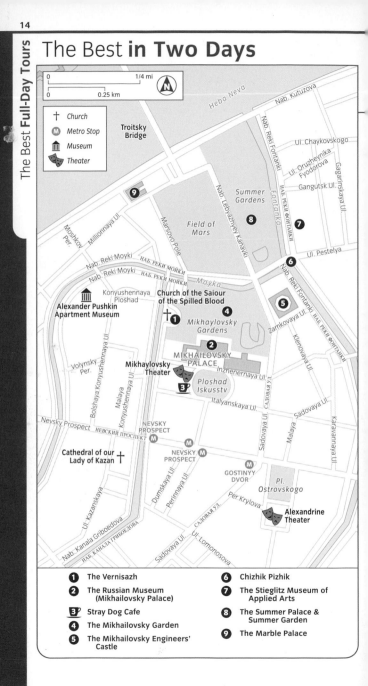

0	1/4 mi
0	0.25 km

† Church
Ⓜ Metro Stop
🏛 Museum
🎭 Theater

Troitsky Bridge

Heba Neva

Nab. Kutuzova

Ul. Chaykovskogo

Nab. Reki Fontanki

Ul. Oruzheynika Fyodorova

Gagarinskaya Ul.

Gangutsk Ul.

НАБ. РЕКИ ФОНТАНКИ

Summer Gardens

Nab. Lebyazhey Kanavki

Фонтанко

Field of Mars

Ul. Pestelya

Moshkov Per.

Millionnaya Ul.

Marsovo Pole

Nab. Reki Moyki   НАБ. РЕКИ МОЙКИ

Nab. Reki Moyki   НАБ. РЕКИ МОЙКИ

Мойка

Nab. Reki Fontanki   НАБ. РЕКИ ФОНТАНКИ

🏛 Alexander Pushkin Apartment Museum

Konyushennaya Ploshad

Church of the Saiour of the Spilled Blood

† ❶

❹

Mikhaylovsky Gardens

Zamkovaya Ul.

❻

❺

❷

MIKHAILOVSKY PALACE

Klenovaya Ul.

Volynsky Per.

Bolshaya Konyushennaya Ul.

Malaya Konyushennaya Ul.

Mikhaylovsky Theater

🎭 ❸

Ploshad Iskusstv

Inzhenernaya Ul.   ИНЖЕНЕРНАЯ УЛ.

Sadovaya Ul.   САДОВАЯ УЛ.

Malaya

Sadovaya Ul.

Karavannaya Ul.

Italyanskaya Ul.

Nevsky Prospect   НЕВСКИЙ ПРОСПЕКТ

NEVSKY PROSPECT Ⓜ

NEVSKY PROSPECT Ⓜ

Cathedral of our Lady of Kazan †

Dumskaya Ul.

Perinnaya Ul.

САДОВАЯ УЛ.

GOSTINYY DVOR Ⓜ

Pl. Ostrovskogo

Per Krylova

Alexandrine Theater 🎭

Ul. Kazanskaya

Nab. Kanala Griboedova   НАБ. КАНАЛА ГРИБОЕДОВА

Sadovaya Ul.

Ul. Lomonosova

❶ The Vernisazh

❷ The Russian Museum (Mikhailovsky Palace)

🎭 ❸ Stray Dog Cafe

❹ The Mikhailovsky Garden

❺ The Mikhailovsky Engineers' Castle

❻ Chizhik Pizhik

❼ The Stieglitz Museum of Applied Arts

❽ The Summer Palace & Summer Garden

❾ The Marble Palace

A day of pure decadence, among the most ornate of the **Romanov** palaces and gardens, exploring the art of the Russian Museum, the statues of the Letniy Sad, and the moats of the Engineers' Castle. START: at the Vernisazh (market) directly behind the Church of the Spilled Blood.

❶ The Vernisazh. Most souvenir tourist-traps pall after about five minutes: but not this one, sandwiched between the Griboedov Canal and the River Moika, overlooking the Mikhailovsky Garden. All the *matroshkas* (Russian nesting dolls), fur hats, and Lenin busts you'd expect, and also amber, mini Fabergé eggs, and Lomonosov porcelain. *Nab. Kanala Griboedova d. 2.* ☎ *812 167 1628. Daily, 9.30am–6pm.*

❷ ★★★ The Russian Museum (Mikhailovsky Palace). See below for the full tour. There are two entrances to this museum, one directly from the Benios Wing on the Griboedov Canal, the other from the Mikhailovsky Palace wing on Ploshad Isskustv. If using the latter, take 10 minutes for an ice-cream or a beer in the shade of the Alexander Pushkin statue, erected in 1957 to commemorate the city's 250th anniversary.

For something more upmarket, go to the Stray Dog Café.

The Mikhailovsky Palace was built in 1819–1835 for the youngest son of Paul I, and opened to the public as the Emperor Alexander III Russian Museum in 1898. This tour is highly selective, covering the best-known masterpieces only, but you should be able to do it in about two hours. Fans of Andrei Rublev, Dionysus, Simon Ushakov and other icon masters should head for Rooms 3 and 4 ❷A–❷B: while the prize exhibits are Rublev's *The Baptism* (1408) and *Apostle Paul* (1408), the most striking piece is Ushakov's *The Old Testament Trinity* (1671). Room 5 ❷C contains some fascinating portraits of Peter the Great: don't miss Carlo Rastrelli's cast of Peter the Great's face, made in 1719, and compare it to Bartolomeo Rastrelli's very different bust beside it,

The Mikhailovsky Palace, home to the Russian Museum.

The Russian Museum

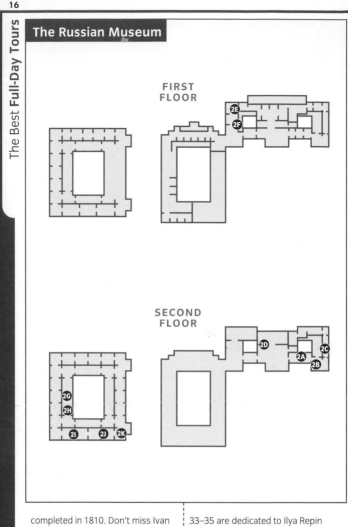

FIRST
FLOOR

SECOND
FLOOR

completed in 1810. Don't miss Ivan Nikitin's *Portrait of Peter I on his Deathbed* (1725). Rooms 5 to 23 cover 19th-century art (there's an interesting portrait of 'Mad' Paul I (V.L. Borovikovskiy, 1800) as you leave the the main gallery in Room 12 **2D**), but things don't get really interesting until you go downstairs to the Rossi Wing, en route to the Avant Gardists in the Benois. Rooms

33–35 are dedicated to Ilya Repin (1844–1930), a leading artist of the Peredvizhniki (or 'Wanderers') school, in revolt against the prevailing classicism of the Academy of Arts. The real masterpieces here are the *Bargemen on the Volga* **2E** (1870–1873) and *Zaporozhe Cossacks Writing a Letter to the Sultan* (1880–1891) **2F**. Once you reach the Benois wing, head straight for

Mikhail Vrubel's works in Rooms 74 and 75, including *Hamlet and Ophelia* (1884), *Flying Demon* (1899) **2G**, and *Morning* (1897) **2H**. Room 78 **2I** has three works by Vasily Kandinsky, *George* (1911), *Picture with Edges* (1919), and *Improvisation* (1910). The Avant Gardists start in Room 80 **2J**, with Alexander Rodchenko's *White Circle* (1918) and *Black on Black* (1918) as well as some more political works on the far wall, and continue into Room 81 with Kazimir Malevich's *Girls in a Field* (1928–1929) and *Suprematism* (1915–1916). ⏱ *2 hrs. Inzhenernaya Ul. d. 4.* ☎ *495 595 4248. www.rusmuseum.ru. Admission to this museum only, 350R adults, 150R kids. Tickets to all branches of the Russian Museum 600R adults, 300R kids. Wed–Mon 10am–6pm, to 5pm Mon.*

3 **Stray Dog Cafe.** A magnet for futurist poets (including Vladimir Mayakovsky and Boris Pasternak), the Stray Dog Cabaret (or Society for Intimate Theater) ran for three years until closed by the authorities in 1915. The sense of history is palpable. Although the service will drive you stark staring mad. *Ploshad Isskustv d. 5/4.* ☎ *812 315 7764. $$$*

4 ★★★ **The Mikhailovsky Garden.** Take five minutes to appreciate the buskers outside the main gates including, if you're lucky, one gifted soul recreating fully harmonized Tchaikovsky on a tray of singing

glasses (see www.crystalharmony.ru). Originally attached to the Summer Palace of Catherine I, the gardens were re-laid in 1823–1825. Admire the Neoclassicism of the Mikhailovsky Palace (the Russian Museum's) rear view, then head north for the Rossi Pavillion (1825) and boat deck. Leave via the gates to the right of the Pavillion and you'll emerge directly opposite the Mikhailovsky (Engineers') Castle, testament to the eccentricity of Catherine the Great's only son, 'Mad' Paul I. *Inzhenernaya Ul. d. 4.* ☎ *495 595 4248. Admission free. Daily, 10am–10pm May–Sept, 10am–8pm Oct–Mar. Closed Apr.*

5 ★ **The Mikhailovsky Castle (Engineers' Castle).** Tsar Paul I's morbid fear of assassination and fascination with the Medieval were combined in this castle (complete with moat and drawbridges), built at the confluence of the Moika and Fontanka rivers. Legends abound, of a secret passage direct from the Royal bedroom, and tunnels carved under the Field of Mars (see p 42). All to no effect. He was murdered by his own guardsmen six weeks after moving in. The statue of Peter the Great in front was erected on the castle's completion (Vincenzo Brenna and Vasily Bazhenov 1797–1800) in 1801: the bas reliefs celebrate the Tsar's victories against the Swedes at Poltava and Hango. The building was given to the army and the Central College of Engineering opened in 1822: students included a 16-year-old Fyodor Dostoevsky, in 1837. It now houses Romanov portrait galleries, Russian folk art and sculpture: worth a

Alexander Pushkin statue on Ploshad Isskustv.

visit if only for a look inside the restored state rooms. *Sadovaya Ul. d. 2.* ☎ *812 570 5112. Admission 300R adults, 150R kids (also includes entry to the Marble Palace and Summer Palace below). Wed–Mon 10am–6pm (to 5pm Mon).*

6 Chizhik Pizhik. You'll see the crowds around this tiny statue as you approach the Panteleimonovsky Bridge: they're trying to throw coins to land on the head of the little metal bird underneath. Its name comes from an old Russian rhyme, a reference to the green-capped students (including a young Pyotr Tchaikovsky) from the Imperial College of Law on the Fontanka Embankment. Seven identical statues have been stolen since the first was installed in 1994.

7 The Stieglitz Museum of Applied Arts. Founded by Baron Alexander von Stieglitz in 1878, its architect (and first director) Maximillian Messmacher's building was inspired by the Italian Renaissance, although individual halls were

Chizhik Pizhik.

The Engineers' Castle.

decorated to match their original contents: don't miss the 18th-century Russian art: inspired by the Terem Palace in the Kremlin. Severely depleted after the Revolution, when many pieces were transferred to the Hermitage, it closed in 1926 before re-opening in 1945. Still used to display works by students of the Central School of Design (for whom it was originally built), its exhibits include glass, ceramics, porcelain and costumes from the 16th–20th centuries. *Solyarny Per. d. 9.* ☎ *812 273 3258. www.stieglitz museum.ru. 120R adults, 50R kids. Tues–Sat 11am–5pm.*

8 The Summer Palace & Summer Garden. The modest, 14-roomed palace is worth visiting as an example of early Petrine architecture (see p 58), or simply to see the private rooms of Peter the Great and his wife, Catherine I. The oldest of the city gardens, the Letniy Sad, was established in 1704 and its layout completed in 1725. While the statues you now see are all copies, they do nonetheless match the 100-plus figures that had been placed in the garden by 1728. Cut through the **Field of Mars** past the **Monument to Revolutionary Fighters** (see p 42) for the Marble Palace. *Letniy Sad.* ☎ *812 312 9666. 10am–10pm, May–Oct, 10am–8pm Oct–Mar. Closed Apr. Summer Palace open Wed–Mon 10am–6pm (to 5pm Mon).*

❾ The Marble Palace. Built by Antonio Rinaldi 1768–1785 for Catherine the Great's favorite (or lover?) Count Orlov, the Marble Palace (so-called for the 32 different types used in its construction) set new standards of opulence, even then. Perhaps the reason the Soviet government chose it to house the History of Material Culture (1919–1936) and, thereafter, a branch of the Lenin Museum. There's a permanent exhibition on *Foreign Artists in Russia*, but the real draw is the modern art in the *Peter Ludwig at the Russian Museum* collection, including works by Andy Warhol.

Statue in the Letniy Sad.

Millionnaya Ul. d. 5/1. ☎ *812 312 9054. Wed–Mon 10am–6pm (to 5pm Mon).*

The Alexander III statue at the Marble Palace.

The Best **in Three Days**

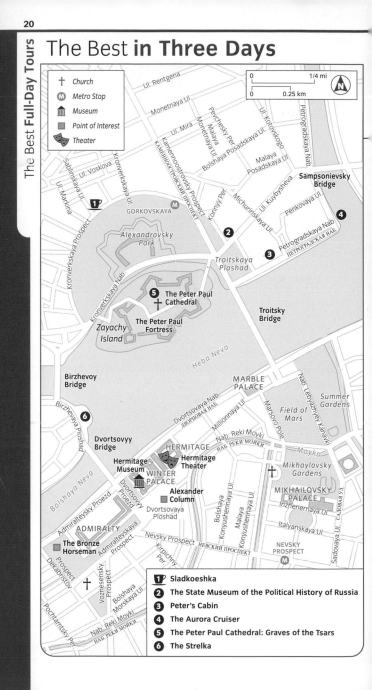

†	Church
Ⓜ	Metro Stop
🏛	Museum
▪	Point of Interest
🎭	Theater

1 Sladkoeshka

2 The State Museum of the Political History of Russia

3 Peter's Cabin

4 The Aurora Cruiser

5 The Peter Paul Cathedral: Graves of the Tsars

6 The Strelka

The Romanov summer palaces (Peterhof, Tsarskoe Tselo) are architecturally stunning and decadent beyond belief: a must see, even on a whistlestop trip (see Chapter 10). If you don't want to go beyond the city, however, the Petrogradsky and Vasilievsky islands north of the River Neva offer plenty to explore. **START: from Gorkovskaya metro, heading south down Kamenoostrovsky Prospect and east into Ulitsa Kuibisheva.**

1 Sladkoeshka. Only for the sweet-toothed, but still worth a visit for the sheer eye-boggling excess of the cakes on sale here. Open from 10am, follow the northern boundary of Alexandrovsky Park for a cup of coffee before you start. *Kronversky Prospect d. 47.* ☎ *812 310 8005. $*

2 ★★★ The State Museum of the Political History of Russia. Housed in the former mansion of Mariinsky prima ballerina Mathilda Kshesinskaya (one of the city's Style Moderne landmarks, see p 105), much of the content does reflect its previous incarnations as a branch of the Central Lenin Museum and, later, the State Museum of the Great October Socialist Revolution. While it covers the key moments in 19th and 20th century Russian history (from the reforms of the 1860s to the events of 1917 and the Russian Civil War), the main draw for non-Russian speakers will be the no-holds-barred 'Soviet Era: Between Utopia and Reality,' tracing the history of repression, propaganda and economic realities from the mid-1920s to perestroika. Don't miss Lenin's office and the office of the Bolshevik Central Committee, kept as they were during the Bolsheviks' occupancy

in April–July 1917, or the video recording of Mikhail Gorbachev under house arrest during the coup of August 1991: and for an insight into Vladimir Putin's rise to power, see the newest collection, 'Russian Politics, With a Petersburg Face.' ⏱ *2 hrs. 2/4 Kuibysheva Ul. d. 2/4.* ☎ *812 449 2833. www.polithistory. ru/en/. Admission 200R adults, 100R kids, tours in English from 250R pp, but call in advance. Daily 10am–6pm, closed Thurs. Metro: Gorkovskaya.*

3 Peter's Cabin. I've almost come to blows with (philistine) friends over this, underwhelmed by the tiny log cabin built in three days by the newly arrived Tsar in May 1703. Although it did not officially become a museum until 1931, its importance was clear almost immediately after Peter's death, its first protective covering being built in 1723 and the interior altered in 1742 to allow easier access for the crowds viewing the Tsar's icon. With sail cloth on the walls, misted 18th century glass in the windows, and an armchair apparently made by the Tsar Carpenter himself, I've always felt it gives a direct sense of the founding fathers' austere and courageous lives. Sceptics, however, point out that the

Peter the Great at Peter's Cabin.

The Aurora Cruiser.

walls are suspiciously IKEA-smooth. ⏱ *30 min. Petrovskaya Nab. d. 6.* ☎ *812 232 4576. www.rusmuseum. ru/eng/. Admission 200R adults, 70R kids. Daily 10am–5pm, closed Tues. Metro: Gorkvoskaya.*

④ ★★★ kids The Aurora Cruiser. Small boys will love this: a real battleship with real guns, and the chance to go below deck to visit the communications and boiler rooms. Its role in the Revolution (see p 39) is legendary— and heavily disputed—some claiming the shots fired to signal the 25th October assault on the Winter Palace were, in fact, blanks. Nonetheless, the cabin from which Lenin broadcast the news of the Bolshevik victory is a must-see. There's a fascinating photo gallery covering its role in the Russo-Japanese War, the Revolution, and the dismantling of its guns for use on the frontline during the Siege of Leningrad (see p 50). With much material in Russian, it's worth taking advantage of any guides that may approach you. Be prepared for steep and narrow staircases: no heels. ⏱ *1 hr. 2/4 Kuibysheva Ul. d. 2/4.* ☎ *812 230 8440. www.aurora.org.ru. Admission free. 10.30am–4pm, closed Mon and Fri. Metro: Gorkovskaya, then tram 2, 6, or 63.*

⑤ ★★★ kids The Peter Paul Cathedral: Graves of the Tsars. Another magnet for small boys, it's worth taking a full day to do justice to the Peter Paul Fortress's prisons, cannon and ghoulish history, particularly if combined with the Artillery Museum directly behind (see p 67 for the full tour). If you're short of

St Petersburg by Helicopter

Prices are eye-wateringly high, but if you've ever dreamt of viewing St Petersburg from the air, it's perfectly possible to arrange. **Baltic Air** run 15-minute flights from the Peter Paul Fortress helipad at 2,000 rubles per person, Sat–Sun only, 12pm–6pm. ☎ 812 704 1676, ☎ 812 571 0084. They run a similar service at Peterhof (see p 162). **Airtours** will fly anywhere you like, any day from Monday to Thursday, starting at €2,100 per hour: they'll take off from the Peter Paul Fortress if you wish, although that's an additional €1,000. ☎ 812 902 9029, ☎ 812 969 6932. www.airtours.spb.ru/ excursions.htm. A number of tour companies offer excursions taking off from Pulkovo: **U-Piter** are among the cheapest, with hire of a four-seater starting at 45,000 rubles per hour. ☎ 812 458 8048, ☎ 8 921 377 5540, ☎ 812 322 9240.

The St Petersburg Metro

Its development put on hold by the exigencies of recovery after the Siege, St Petersburg's first metro line (the Kirovsko–Vyborskaya (red)) did not open until 1955—two years after Stalin's death, when Khrushchev was already cutting back on the worst excesses of the earlier regime. As a result, only this line comes close to matching the glamour of the Moscow metro, but its central stations do not disappoint. **Ploshad Vosstania** is said to have the last remaining sculpture of Stalin (see p 42); and look closely at the sculptured panel you'll see above the escalators at **Narvskaya**: the characters seem to be encircling (and looking at) a blank space. Urban myth has it that a figure of Stalin was due to be placed here—never completed, for reasons of either death or dishonor. The station does, apparently, have a panel of Stalin, hidden behind a false wall in 1961. **Avtovo** is currently undergoing restoration, but the floor-to-ceiling cut glass on the pillars is still impressive, as is the sheer volume of granite, running from the cupola-topped ticket hall to the platforms.

time, however, head for the Peter Paul Cathedral, burial place of almost all members of the Romanov dynasty. Peter the Great is here, as are Catherine II, Nicholas and Alexandra, and the children of the last Imperial family, re-interred in 1998. While the original cathedral was consecrated directly after the founding of the city (in 1704), this building was completed in 1733. Don't miss the iconostasis—an icon-filled tower rather than the typical layered screen—and try to time your visit for the daily cannon shot (from the Naryshkin Bastion) at noon.

Ploshad Vosstaniya metro.

The Rostoral Columns.

🕐 *1 hr.* ☎ *812 230 232 9454. Admission to the cathedral only 150R adults, 70R kids. Daily 10am–8pm. Access to the belltower is possible at certain times (closed Wed), at 150R adults, 60R kids. Metro:*

The Strelka.

Gorkovskaya, then marshrutka (minibus) Nos 46, 76, 183, 223, bus No. 6 or tram No. 46. Tram No. 6 also runs from the Avrora (see above).

❻ ★★★ The Strelka. It's a long walk from the Peter Paul Fortress to the Strelka (the eastern-most spit of Vasilievsky Island), but worth it for the views of the Palace Embankment, Birzhevaya Ploshad (Exchange Square) and, if you time it right, floodlight fountains as you cross the Birzhevoy Bridge. This is one spot definitely to be visited during White Nights, when—during the annual Economic Forum or *Aliye Parusa* end of term street party—flares are lit from the top of the Rostoral Columns and lasers shoot across the facades of the Winter Palace. If you're still on your feet, follow Birzhevoy Proezd eastwards and wander the statue-lined Mendeleyevskaya Liniya and the Twelve Colleges, built between 1722–1742 to house Peter the Great's various ministries, now part of St Petersburg State University. See the full Vasilievsky Island tour on p 78. ●

Hermitage: **The State Rooms**

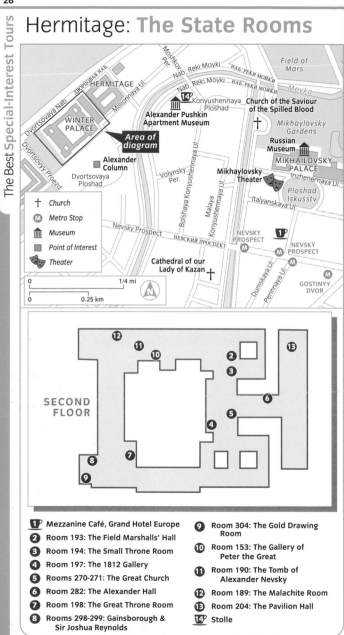

† Church
Ⓜ Metro Stop
🏛 Museum
🟩 Point of Interest
🎭 Theater

Mezzanine Café, Grand Hotel Europe
Room 193: The Field Marshalls' Hall
Room 194: The Small Throne Room
Room 197: The 1812 Gallery
Rooms 270-271: The Great Church
Room 282: The Alexander Hall
Room 198: The Great Throne Room
Rooms 298-299: Gainsborough & Sir Joshua Reynolds
Room 304: The Gold Drawing Room
Room 153: The Gallery of Peter the Great
Room 190: The Tomb of Alexander Nevsky
Room 189: The Malachite Room
Room 204: The Pavilion Hall
Stolle

Isn't this the reason you're here? And it doesn't disappoint. After 15 years, and more visits than I can count, I still take Rastrelli's Jordan Staircase two at a time. But go in the afternoon. Even if you manage to dodge the summer queues with an online booking (see p 166) you'll still face troops of schoolchildren being drilled on Renaissance art. While always referred to as 'The Hermitage', the world's greatest art gallery was in fact built by successive Romanov rulers, beginning with the Baroque Winter Palace built by Peter the Great's daughter Elizaveta Petrovna. The following mini-tours have been designed to take you straight to the must-sees of each of the main collections, in around two hours. This one begins with the Winter Palace's most grandiose State Rooms, ending with Catherine the Great's Pavillion Hall, connecting to her Neoclassical Great Hermitage. START: **at the Field Marshalls' Hall, left at the top of the Jordan Staircase.**

1⃣ Mezzanine Café, Grand Hotel Europe. There's a branch of Internet chain Cafe Max within the Hermitage, as well as its own (hopelessly crowded) buffet. But why compromise? You'll find surprisingly good value all-day breakfasts at the Mezzannine Café, including salmon and poached eggs or omelets, from

400 rubles. *Mikhailovskaya Ulitsa d. 1/7.* ☎ *812 329 6000. $$.*

2⃣ Room 193: The Field Marshalls' Hall. The building you are walking through is not the original Winter Palace: that was built for Peter I in 1712. This version, which remained the main residence of the

The Winter Palace.

Illustration of the Jordan Staircase.

Imperial Family until the Revolution of February 1917, was built by Francesco Bartolomeo Rastrelli for Peter the Great's daughter Empress Elizaveta Petrovna, begun in 1754 and continuing, after her death, to 1762. Directly left from the Jordan Staircase, go through the Field Marshalls' Hall (the starting point of the devastating fire of 1837) to the Small Throne Room and the Armorial Hall: all part of the Grand Suite, redesigned by Vasily Stasov following the fire. A word to the wise: the restrooms downstairs from the ticket office have interminable queues. Those directly under the Jordan Staircase, however, are almost always empty.

❸ ★★★ **Room 194: The Small Throne Room.** Originally designed by Auguste de Montferrand in 1833, the painting above the Romanov throne shows Peter I with Minerva, goddess of wisdom. Take a close look at the chandeliers in the neighboring **Armorial Hall** (Rm. 195): slotted in among the lights are the arms and emblems of all the Russian provinces.

❹ **Room 197: The 1812 Gallery.** Alexander I's homage to the military leaders of the 1812 Patriotic War: Mikhail Kutuzov (responsible for the razing of Moscow after defeat at the Battle of Borodino, and Napoleon's ultimate withdrawal) is on the left of the door facing you: Barclay de Tolly (the minister for war) is on the right.

❺ **Rooms 270–271: The Great Church.** Originally designed by Bartolomeo Rastrelli, Vasily Stasov remained faithful to that earlier work during restoration after the fire of 1837. It was here that the last of the Romanovs, Nicholas II, married Alix of Hess in 1894. Don't miss the ceiling painting, *The Ascension of Christ*, by Pyotr Basin.

❻ **Room 282: The Alexander Hall.** Restored in 2007, this room, named for Tsar Alexander I, commemorates his victories in the Patriotic War of 1812 and the subsequent European Campaigns. Twenty-four medallions record the major events of those conflicts.

❼ **Room 198: The Great Throne Room.** Also known as the St George Hall for the bas relief above the throne, the most 'Imperial' of the state rooms suffered badly during the Revolution, and was used for one of the most 'Soviet' exhibits thereafter, with the Tsarist symbols removed and replaced with a map of the USSR, made from semi-precious stones.

❽ **Rooms 298–299: Gainsborough & Sir Joshua Reynolds.** From here I always make a pretty swift dash straight for the Gold Drawing Room. Brits, however, won't want to miss Gainsborough's *Lady in Blue* (c.1780) in Rm. 299, nor two works by Sir Joshua Reynolds, *The Infant Hercules Strangling the Serpents* (1786–1788) and *Cupid Untying the Zone of Venus* (1788), in Rm. 300.

9 ★★★ Room 304: The Gold Drawing Room. Cut through Rms.167–168 for a look at the deliciously rococo boudoir of Maria Alexandrovna, wife of Alexander II, before heading left for this gilt extravaganza, originally designed by Alexander Briullov in 1838–1841 and refurbished by Eclecticist architect Andrei Stakenschneider in the 1840s. Don't miss the mosaic panel above the fireplace, *The Ruins of Paestum*, by Gioacchino Rinaldi.

10 Room 153: The Gallery of Peter the Great. Effectively the Romanov family album, notable in particular for two works by Russian artists of the Peredvizniki (Wanderers) school: Ilya Repin's *Portrait of Nicholas II* (1895) and Ivan Kramskoi's *Empress Maria Fedorovna* (1881).

11 Room 190: The Tomb of Alexander Nevsky. Commissioned by Peter the Great's daughter and heir Elizabeth Petrovna, and made in the St Petersburg mint 1747–1752, this 1.5-ton silver edifice was transferred from the Alexander Nevsky Monastery in 1922. You'll notice two photos of the ill-fated Nicholas II and Alexandra, taken in 1903 when this hall hosted a sumptuous fancy dress ball: the Tsar and Tsarina appearing in the traditional costumes shown here. Nicholas II's costume apparently contained so many jewels it was retained thereafter in the Kremlin Armory.

12 ★★★ Room 189: The Malachite Room. Designed by Alexander Briullov after the fire of 1837 as the personal drawing room of the wife of Nicholas I, the last meeting of the Provisional Government took place here on October 25th, 1917. The government was later arrested in the adjoining Small Dining Room.

13 ★★★ Room 204: The Pavilion Hall. Connecting the Petrine Baroque Winter Palace with the Neoclassical Great Hermitage, this room (part of the Small Hermitage and designed by Andrei Stakenschneider) features recreations of a Roman mosaic floor, and the Fountains of Bakhtchisaray. The real must-see, however, is the **Peacock Clock**, given to Catherine the Great by her lover Grigori Potemkin in 1791. It is wound only rarely: see it in action at closedown on the Kultura Channel.

14 Stolle. A 21st-century take on the traditional pirozhkovaya (pie shop), i.e., far cleaner and with better service. The sheer range here is staggering, both sweet and savory: choose from salmon, rabbit, fish, herring, cranberry, cherry or apricot. *Konushenny Per. d. 1/6.* ☎ *812 312 1862.* $.

Illustration featuring the Peacock Clock.

Exploring the **Hermitage**

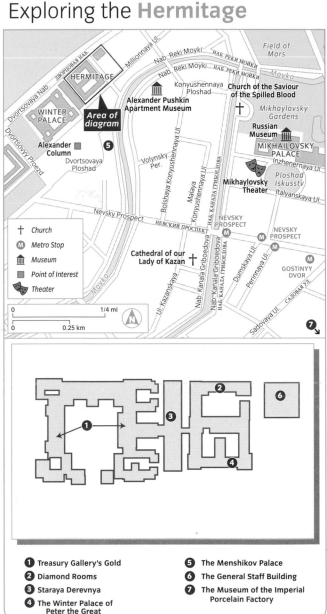

1 Treasury Gallery's Gold

2 Diamond Rooms

3 Staraya Derevnya

4 The Winter Palace of Peter the Great

5 The Menshikov Palace

6 The General Staff Building

7 The Museum of the Imperial Porcelain Factory

The Hermitage: Need to Know

Book online. Not only will you receive a discounted two-day ticket, including admission to all branches, but you'll be exempt from having to queue. But bizarrely, online tickets are processed in the USA, and can take up to three days to come through (www.hermitagemuseum.org). One-day tickets are $17.95, two-day tickets $25.95. If you do find yourself making an impromptu visit in summer, make sure you're in the queue before 9.30am (an hour before it opens) or leave it until well after lunch. Otherwise, expect a wait of up to an hour at peak times. Open-air cafés and chemical toilets appear in the courtyard every summer: you'll find your place is kept for you if you need to use them.

Costs. Admission is free for all students and children, regardless of nationality. Adults (foreigners) are charged 350R, except on the last Thursday of every month when it's free for all. Branch museums (see below) can be visited individually, at 200R each. ☎ **812 571 8446**. Admission to the ❶ **Treasury Gallery's Gold** and ❷ **Diamond Rooms** is only possible as part of a group tour, at a further 300R each. You'll find times listed at the ticket office.

❸ **Staraya Derevnya.** The Hermitage depository (holding paintings and exhibits not on display) is now open to the public, although only as part of a tour, booked in advance. ***Zausadebnaya Ulitsa, d, 37-A.*** ☎ **812 344 9226**. 200R.

❹ **The Winter Palace of Peter the Great.** It had been assumed that Peter I's 1712 palace had been destroyed in the building of the Hermitage Theater. Research conducted in the 1970s–1980s, however, revealed a large part of the former courtyard beneath the theater's stage, as well as the remains of Peter I's private chambers. This exhibition, covering his life and times, opened in 1992. ***Dvortsovaya Pl. d. 32.***

❺ **The Menshikov Palace.** See p 80.

❻ **The General Staff Building.** Carlo Rossi's 1827 Neoclassical masterpiece hosts exhibitions on Tsarist military history, as well as the works of Post-Impressionists Pierre Bonnard and Maurice Denis, and Russian Art Nouveau. ***Dvortsovaya Pl. d. 6/8.***

❼ **The Museum of the Imperial Porcelain Factory.** Collections from the Imperial Factory since the 18th century. Placed under the control of the People's Commissariat for Education after the Revolution, the 1920s–1930s collections are stunning. ***Obukhovskoi Oborony Prospect d. 151.*** ☎ **812 326 4620.**

The Hermitage: Grandmasters

† Church

🏛 Museum

⬛ Point of Interest

❶ Rooms 262-258: Pieter Brueghel the Younger

❷ Room 247: Pieter Paul Rubens

❸ Rembrandt Harmensz van Rijn

☕ Tea Room, Kempinski Moika Hotel

While Peter I first brought Rembrandt to Russia, Catherine the Great's purchase of Dutch Grandmasters from the bankrupt Johann Ernst Gotzkowsky in 1764 began what was to become the world's greatest collection of European art. Yuri Velten was commissioned to build the Small Hermitage (1765–1766) and later the Great Hermitage (1771–1787) to hold her ever-expanding collection. The New Hermitage (the only part of the complex designed as a public art gallery) was added in 1851 by Nicholas I. The real gems are here, in the Rubens and Rembrandt rooms: but don't miss the works of Pieter Brueghel the Younger, just beyond the Romanov Gallery. **START:** with the Jordan Staircase behind you, head west through the Trophy Art (p 36), turning right into the Romanov Gallery (Rm. 259).

❶ Rooms 262–258: Pieter Brueghel the Younger. You'll find one of the best known works, *The Adoration of the Magi,* on your right, and another, *Kermis,* on the opposite side. The last of the Brueghel works, *Robbers Attacking the Peasants,* is in Rm. 258. You will

also find works by his brother Jan Brueghel the Elder (both the sons of Pieter Brueghel the Elder), in **Rm. 248**, just before reaching the Rubens Room.

❷ ★★★ Room 247: Pieter Paul Rubens. A cluster of famous

Detail of Bacchus by Rubens.

early works can be found on the right-hand side of the far end of the room: *Susannah and the Elders* (1607), *Ecce Homo* (c.1610) and *Adoration of the Shepherds* (c. 1615–1616). Opposite is one of his most famous later works, *Bacchus* (1638–1640), unmissable on the left-hand side as you walk in. Retrace your steps through to **Rm. 249** for **Jan Steen's** *The Revellers*, en route to the Rembrandt room.

❸ ★★★ Rembrandt Harmensz van Rijn. Originally modelled on his wife Saskia (although later changed to show the face of his mistress Geertje Dircs), Rembrandt's *Danae* (1636–1640) is unmissable among the other 20 of his works lining the left-hand wall. Other must-sees include *The Adoration of the Magi* (1632), *The Holy Family* (1645), *Portrait of an Old Man in Red* (1652–1654), and *The Return of the Prodigal Son* (1668–1669). Somewhat out of chronological order, the last piece you will see as you leave is *Abraham's Sacrifice*, (1635).

❹ Tea Room, Kempinski Moika Hotel. Finish off a day of elegance and luxury with cucumber sandwiches and English High Tea. *Nab Reki Moiki d. 22.* ☎ *812 335 9111.* *$$$.*

Adoration of the Magi by Brueghel the Younger.

34

The Hermitage: Italian Renaissanc

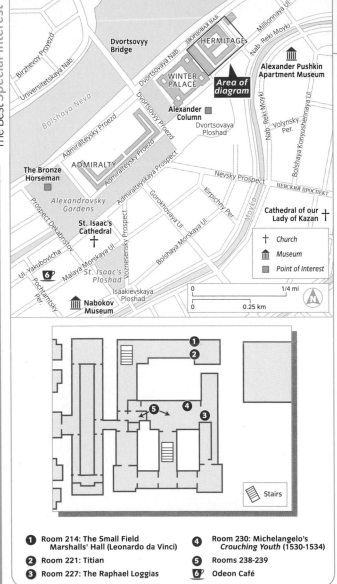

1. Room 214: The Small Field Marshalls' Hall (Leonardo da Vinci)

2. Room 221: Titian

3. Room 227: The Raphael Loggias

4. Room 230: Michelangelo's *Crouching Youth* (1530-1534)

5. Rooms 238-239

6. Odeon Café

Covering five centuries and 30 rooms, the Hermitage's collection of Italian painting includes works by Caravaggio, Fran Angelico, and Raphael in addition to the famous names shown below. Be warned: these exhibitions attract an implausible number of tour groups and schoolchildren. Go very early, or very late.

START: **at Fra Angelico's Madonna and Child, in Room 207.**

1 ★★★ **Room 214: The Small Field Marshalls' Hall (Leonardo da Vinci).** So-called for the medallions of famous soldiers that decorate the walls (Napoleonic war hero, Kutuzov is above the door as you enter, victor of the Turkish campaigns Suvorov as you leave), it was here that Nicholas I interrogated the leaders of the Decembrist Uprising of 1825. Most visitors, however, will be here to see Leonardo da Vinci's *Madonna and Child* (the Benois Madonna, c. 1478) and the Litta Madonna (c. 1481–1497).

2 ★★★ **Room 221: Titian.** Five of the pieces on display here (including *St Sebastian* (1570s) and *The Penitent Mary Magdelene* (c. 1560s)) were acquired from the collection of the palace of Cristoforo Barbarigo (where Titian had died in 1576). Must-sees include *Danae* (c. 1550s), the *Portrait of Pope Paul III*, *Christ Carrying the Cross* (c. 1560s), and *The Flight Into Egypt.* (early 1500s).

3 ★★★ **Room 227: The Raphael Loggias.** The Large Hermitage was extended in 1792 to house this gallery, an almost identical reproduction of the Raphael Loggias in the Vatican, produced for Catherine the Great by architect Giacomo Quarenghi and painted by artists under the direction of Christopher Unterberger.

4 ★★★ **Room 230: Michelangelo's *Crouching Youth* (1530–1534).** While this exhibition does contain 17 sketches and studies by Michelangelo Buonarroti, this is the only genuine sculpture in the country, originally intended for the Medici Chapel, Florence.

5 kids **Rooms 238–239.** Entirely unrelated to Italian art, a detour here will reveal mounted knights and suits of armor, some dating from the 15th century, in the **Ritsevsky Hall** (Rm. 238), and four paintings by **Diego Velazquez**, including two portraits of Philip II of Spain (1656–1660), in Rm. 239.

6 **Odeon Café.** A new (and promising) opening in December 2008: red leather sofas, gilt mirrors, decadent cakes (made on the premises) and perfect Italian coffee. *Ul. Yakubovitcha d. 10.* ☎ *812 710 6932. $.*

The Litta Madonna by Leonardo da Vinci.

The Hermitage: The Impressionists

- **1** Rooms 146-143: Trophy Art
- **1A** Room 146
- **1B** Room 145
- **1C** Room 144
- **1D** Room 143
- **2** Room 257: Vasily Kandinsky
- **3** Rooms 314-344: The Impressionists
- **3A** Room 318: Cezanne's *Self Portrait* (1873)
- **3B** Room 318: Van Gogh
- **3C** Room 316: Paul Gaugin
- **3D** Room 319: Monet's *Waterloo Bridge* (1903)
- **3E** Room 344: Henri Matisse's *The Dance* (1910)
- **4** Rooms 348-349: Pablo Picasso
- **5** James Cook

Don't rush straight to the main Impressionist collection (and the Picassos) on the third floor. The best of the 'Trophy Art' Impressionist collection—and all of the Kandinskys—are on the floor below. START: **with the Jordan Staircase behind you, heading west through Room 200 for the Trophy Art.**

1 ★★★ **Rooms 146–143: Trophy Art.** The text at the entrance is such a masterful piece of understatement it has to be translated in full: 'Works from private collections from Germany, transferred after WWII'. While Germany maintains that many of the works taken by the victorious Russian troops are museum pieces which should be returned, Roskhrankultura (part of the Ministry of Culture) remains adamant they are reasonable recompense for Russia's losses during the war, and will not be returned without compensation. But don't miss it: I remember the excitement when these works, in storage for decades, were finally put on display for the first time in 1994. Rm. 146 **1A** contains works by Edgar Degas, including *The Dancer* (1874), and Rm. 145 **1B** has four works by Camille Pissarro, as well as a still life by Auguste Renoir. Renoir works continue in Rms. 145 (which also contains Claude Monet's *The Seine at Rouen* (1872)), and Rm. 144 **1C**.

The must-see in Rm. 144, however, is Paul Cezanne's *Self Portrait* (1880–1881). The final hall, Rm. 143 **1D** contains Gaugin's *Piti Teina* (1892), and *Ballerina* by Henri Matisse, but the real draw here is the four Van Gogh works, including *Landscape with Horse and Plough* (1889).

2 ★★★ **Room 257: Vasily Kandinsky.** The quickest way from the Trophy Art is via the Western Gallery (Medieval European art, and left through the 15th–16th-century Netherlands collection in Rm. 258. The right-hand side as you enter has *View of Murnau* (1908), *Landscape* (1913) and *Winter* (1909). Retrace your steps through Rm. 258, and bear left through the collection in Rms. 263–268: you'll find yourself at the staircase leading to the main Impressionists collection on the third floor.

3 **Rooms 314–344: The Impressionists.** The real gems begin with Cezanne's *Self Portrait* (1873) in Rm. 318 **3A**, leading into four Van Gogh's (including *Arena at Arles* (1868)) in Rm. 318 **3B**. Rm. 316 **3C** is devoted to the work of Paul

Gaugin, including *Woman Holding a Fruit* (1893) and *Women by the* Sea (1899). Rm. 319 contains works by Claude Monet and Auguste Rodin's sculpture, *Cupid and Psyche* (1905). The must-see in Rm. 319 **3D** is Claude Monet's *Waterloo Bridge* (1903), but probably the most famous piece of the collection is in Rm. 344 **3E**: Henri Matisse's *The Dance* (1910), acquired (somewhat forcibly) after the Revolution from the private collection of industrialist Sergei Shchukin.

4 **Rooms 348–349: Pablo Picasso.** Considered eccentric for his early support of the Impressionists, Shchukin also collected early Picassos, many of them on display here, including *Violin and Guitar* (1912–1913). There's a piece from the Blue Period (*Two Sisters* (1902)), and many Cubist pieces, including *Woman with a Fan* (1907–1908).

5 **James Cook.** Much-loved expat haunt, perfect for a beer while catching the late afternoon sun. *Schvedsky Per. d. 3* ☎ *812 312 3200. $.*

The Arena at Arles by Vincent Van Gogh.

Bolsheviks & Revolutionaries

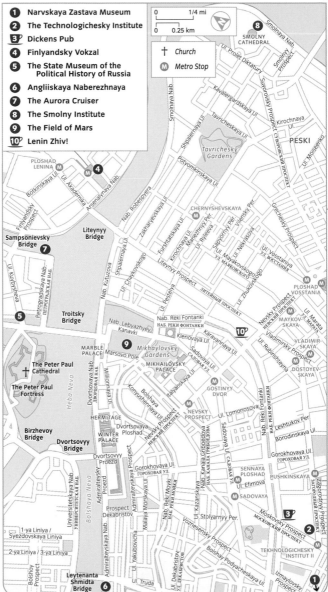

1 Narvskaya Zastava Museum
2 The Technologichesky Institute
3 Dickens Pub
4 Finlyandsky Vokzal
5 The State Museum of the Political History of Russia
6 Angliiskaya Naberezhnaya
7 The Aurora Cruiser
8 The Smolny Institute
9 The Field of Mars
10 Lenin Zhiv!

0   1/4 mi
0   0.25 km

† Church
Ⓜ Metro Stop

he Tsarist capital was home to the country's revolutionaries long before the Great October Revolution of 1917. The Petrashevsky Circle (of which Dostoevsky was the most famous member) hoped for an end to Tsarist autocracy and serfdom, and the *Narodnaya Volya* (People's Will) movement used terrorist tactics (including assassinating Alexander II) to try to secure an elected legislature and universal suffrage. As rapid industrialization at the end of the 19th century gave rise to an increasingly radicalized working class, military failure coinciding with economic hardship resulted in the uprisings of 1905 and 1917: the latter triggering the events which were to change the country and the world. This tour uncovers some of the lesser-known sites central to the development of the revolutionary movement, but follows a chronological order rather than a geographically convenient one. If you're short of time, the Narvskaya Zastava museum, the Field of Mars and the Smolny Institute are the 'must sees'. START: **at Ul. Ivana Chernykh for the Narvskaya Zastava Museum, first left after the metro.**

❶ ★★★ Narvskaya Zastava Museum. At first sight this museum is underwhelming. The hall on your left offers a very mundane recreation of pre-revolutionary middle-class life (something the Yelizarov Museum does far better, see p 53). But persevere: it has photographs of pre-revolutionary working-class Petrograd which you are unlikely to see anywhere else. You'll find pictures of a fresh-faced Vladimir Ulyanov (Lenin) together with other members of the 'St Petersburg Union for the Struggle of the Working Class' (see below), as well as Sergei Witte, head of Nicholas II's first Council of Ministers and author of the 1905 October Manifesto, the first concession to constitutional and elected government. Ask the attendants to point out Bloody Sunday march leader turned agent provocateur Father Georgy Gapon, pictured with workers from the Putilovsky factory in December 1904, and don't miss the photos of the Bloody Sunday marchers on Prospect Stachek. Nor of the Cossack troops who so brutally crushed them. *Narvskaya Zastava Museum.*

Ul. Ivana Chernikh d. 23. ☎ *812 252 1341. Admission 100R adults, 50R kids. Mon–Fri 10am–5pm (to 4pm Fri). Metro: Narvskaya.*

❷ ★★ The Technologichesky Institute. Its origins remain in dispute, but according to Leon Trotsky at least, the first meeting of what was to become the **St Petersburg Soviet of Workers' Deputies** took

The Technologichesky Institute.

Kirovsky Zavod

This site might be more conveniently visited as part of the Workers' Paradise tour of Prospect Stachek (see p 82), but no guide of the city's key revolutionary landmarks would be complete without it. Crucial to the revolutions of both 1905 and 1917, the Kzenniy Chugunoliteiny (cast iron) factory was founded in 1801 under Tsar Paul I. Acquired by Nikolai Putilov in 1868, by 1910 it had a workforce of 30,000 (the largest in Russia) and, under the leadership of Mikhail Kalinin and Grigory Zinoviev had become central to the burgeoning workers' movement. The dismissal of four Putilovsky workers in December 1904 led to the strike which was ultimately to paralyze the entire city and lead to the Bloody Sunday march on the Winter Palace, on 9th January, 1905. Due to convene on Palace Square at 2pm, the largest of the marches from the Putilovsky works came under fire as soon as it reached the Narvskaya Gate. *Kirovsky Zavod, Prospect Stachek d. 47.* ☎ *812 702 0409. www. kzgroup.ru. Metro: Kirovsky Zavod.*

place here on 13th October 13th, 1905. Initially headed by Georgy Khrustalyov-Nosar, Trotsky assumed leadership on Nosar's arrest in November; the organization was dissolved a month later when troops stormed the building to arrest Trotsky. *Moskovsky Prospect d. 25. Metro: Technologichesky Institute.*

3⃣ Dickens Pub. This is a long tour. Before you go any further grab one of the all-day breakfasts on offer here, just a short walk north up Moskovsky Prospect, turning right onto the Fontanka. *Nab. Reki Fontanki d. 108.* ☎ *812 380 7998. $$.*

4⃣ ★★ Finlyandsky Vokzal. Locomotive No. 293, in which a heavily disguised Lenin made his return in April 1917, still stands on the platform at Finlyandsky Vokzal, these days under a protective glass case. Panels in the ceiling of the main hall depict the main events of the Revolution, and a massive

statue on Ploshad Lenina (directly in front of the station) shows the eponymous hero declaiming to the masses. While here, you might want to make a detour to nearby **21 Komsomola Street**, home of the St. Petersburg Union for the Struggle of the Working Class.

Lenin at Finlyandsky Vokzal.

The Smolny Institute.

Founded in 1895 with members including Lenin and his future wife Nadezhda Krupskaya, the group later merged with others to become the Russian Social Democratic Labor Party, from which the Bolshevik and Menshevik factions were to evolve. *Finlyandsky Vokzal, Ploshad Lenina d. 6. Metro: Ploshad Lenina.*

⑤ ★★★ The State Museum of the Political History of Russia. The Bolshevik headquarters from March–July 1917. *See p 21.*

⑥ ★★ Angliiskaya Naberezhnaya. Site of the *Avrora*'s mooring when it gave the signal to attack the Winter Palace. At least according to some. *Angliiskaya Naberezhnaya d. 44. Metro: Sadovaya, then marshrutki 350, 124, 186 to Ploshad Truda.*

⑦ ★★ The Aurora Cruiser. At this point it becomes very difficult to separate history and myth. Some claim the *Avrora* opened fire on the Winter Palace, others that it merely fired blanks to give the signal to attack. Still others claim it was not even moored in the Neva on the night of the great events. Suspend disbelief and see for yourself (p 22).

⑧ ★★ The Smolny Institute. This isn't an easy museum to visit since Smolny remains the center of the City Government and security is, of necessity, strict. But the Museum Director assures me it is accessible at any time to those booking in advance. The superbly informed guides will point out the exact spot from which Lenin addressed the 2nd All-Russia Congress of Soviets in the Assembly Hall, the third-floor corridor in which St Petersburg party chief Sergei Kirov was shot (directly opposite room 356), and the first floor office in which a young Vladimir Putin cut his teeth as the protégé of the reformist Mayor Anatoly Sobchak (in what are now offices 112–116). The headquarters of the Bolshevik Petrograd Soviet in 1917, this was the center of government until the capital was transferred to Moscow in 1918, and Lenin's living

Where's Lenin?

Most of the old Soviet statues were torn down in the exuberant early 1990s, but you can still find him in front of the **Dom Sovetov** (Moskovsky Prospect d. 212, metro: Moskovskaya), at the **Alexandrovsky Lycee** (Kamennoostrovsky Prospect d. 21, metro: Petrogradskaya), at the top of Ulitsa Lenina (Petrogradskaya, see p 53) and at **Findlyandsky Vokzal**. Images of Stalin have been almost completely eradicated, but walk the length of the platform from the downward escalator at **Ploshad Vostanniya** metro, to the final brass plaque on the right. Who is that moustachioed man behind Lenin? Whatever one's feelings about the subject matter, the Isaac Brodsky museum holds some classic pieces of socialist realist art. *The Isaac Brodsky Museum, Ploshad Isskustv d. 3.* ☎ *812 314 3658. www.nimrah.ru. Closed Mon–Tues. Metro: Gostiny Dvor.*

quarters during that time are a must-see. More poignant, however, are the photos taken in the first winter of the Revolution, with a fresh-faced Joseph Stalin standing shoulder to shoulder with Lenin: neither aware of the course the Revolution would take after his death. *Ploshad Rastrelli d. 3/1.* ☎ *812 576 7461. Admission by prior arrangement only, 300R adults, 200R kids.*

The Dom Sovetov.

9 ★★ **The Field of Mars.** Originally laid out as gardens for Empress Elizabeth, and later as a parade ground during construction of the neighboring Mikhailovsky Castle, this park took on its current use in 1917, when the victims of the 1905 revolution were re-interred here. Victims of the 1917 Revolution and the Civil War followed, with a Memorial to the Victims of

the Revolution erected in 1917. The current Memorial to Revolutionary Fighters (which holds the country's first Eternal Flame) was erected in 1957.

10 **Lenin Zhiv!** The city has numerous 'Soviet Kitsch' bars these days, but this is among the cheapest, and the most central. If you like this you'll love NEP and Purga. *Nab. Reki Fontanki d. 4* ☎ *812 275 3558. $$.*

The memorial to revolutionary fighters at the Field of Mars.

The Revolutionary City

St Petersburg's revolutionary history can be confusing: there were two in 1917 alone. The key events to remember are:

The Revolution of 1905: Against a background of economic depression and disaster in the Russo-Japanese War (1904–1905), strikes and unrest led ultimately to the massacre of Bloody Sunday on January 9th, 1905. Unrest spread throughout the country (including the mutiny on the battleship *Potemkin* in June), culminating in the General Strike of October 1905, directed by the St Petersburg Soviet of Workers' Deputies. Under pressure from Sergei Witte, President of his 1905 Council of Ministers, Nicholas II's October Manifesto finally promised an elected Duma and a constitution.

The February Revolution of 1917: A disastrous campaign in WWI and food riots in Petrograd forced Nicholas II to abdicate on February 24th. A power struggle between the (Tsarist) Provisional Government and the Petrograd Soviet of Workers' and Soldiers' Deputies ended with the issuing of the Soviet's Order No.1 in March, asserting its authority over the military. The first All-Russian Congress of People's Soviets (comprising Socialist Revolutionaries, Bolsheviks and Mensheviks) took place on June 3rd, but the Provisional Government held until October as a summer coup by the soviets (the 'July Days') failed and Lenin fled to Finland. The regional soviets became increasingly powerful, however, and by September the Bolsheviks had taken control of those in St Petersburg and Moscow. The Military Revolutionary Committee of the Petrograd Soviet was formed on October 20th. Under its direction, key buildings—including the Winter Palace—were captured on October 25th. The *Avrora* fired blank shots as the signal to attack, and the Red Guard stormed the Winter Palace. The Second All-Russian Congress of Soviets took place the next day.

Literary **Landmarks**

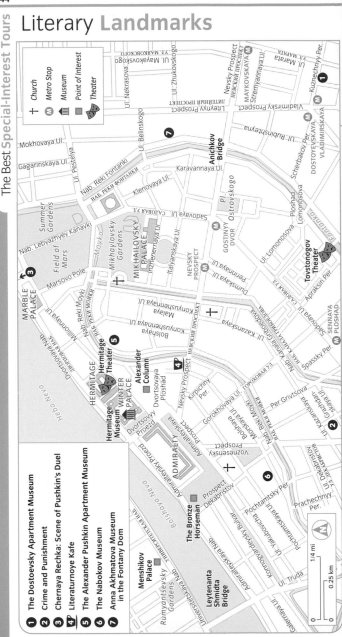

1 The Dostoevsky Apartment Museum

2 Crime and Punishment

3 Chernaya Rechka: Scene of Pushkin's Duel

4 Literaturnoye Kafe

5 The Alexander Pushkin Apartment Museum

6 The Nabokov Museum

7 Anna Akhmatova Museum in the Fontany Dom

+ Church

Ⓜ Metro Stop

🏛 Museum

▪ Point of Interest

🎭 Theater

This very demanding tour could well take you an entire day, retracing the key events in the (eccentric and adventurous) lives of the country's greatest writers, Pushkin and Dostoevsky. Modernists might prefer to head straight for the Nabokov and Akhmatova museums, while historians can re-examine the city's early revolutionary history in the sites of Dostoevsky's various arrests. **START: at the Dostoevsky Apartment Museum, his final residence and the scene of his death.**

❶ The Dostoevsky Apartment Museum.

Fyodor Dostoevsky (1821–1881) lived in this apartment for two years before his death, completing *The Brothers Karamazov* during that time. The museum is divided into two sections: his working quarters, and his family apartments, the latter, in particular, a painstaking recreation of turn-of-the-century life, filled with personal artefacts and photos. *Kuznechny Per. d. 5/2.* ☎ *812 571 4031. www.md.spb.ru. Admission 120R. Tues–Sun 11am–6pm. Metro: Vladimirskaya, Dostoevskaya.*

❷ Crime and Punishment.

As well as touring the main sites of Dostoevsky's life (below), you might also like to cover the key locations of one of his greatest novels, set around Sennaya Ploshad: now home to some of the city's biggest malls, but once the haunt of itinerants and down-and-outs. A statue of Dostoevsky stands in front of **Stolarny Pereulok d. 5,** said to be the location of the apartment of the novel's murdererous anti-hero Rodion Raskolnikov, although others claim the real location is at d. 9. Either way, following Raskolnikov's '730 steps will lead you to the house of his victim, the elderly moneylender, at **Prospect Rimskovo-Korsakova d. 25**, passing heroine Sonya Marmeladova's house en route at **Nab. Kanal Griboedova d. 73**.

❸ Chernaya Rechka: Scene of Pushkin's Duel.

Alexander Pushkin (1799–1837, the Russian Romantic poet, considered the founder of modern Russian literature) married society beauty Natalya Goncharova in 1831. Driven mad by rumors of an affair with George d'Anthès in 1837, he challenged him to a duel on 8th February, dying from wounds two days later. Only the most committed fans will want to make the long trek north to the scene of the poet's untimely demise, but if you're one of them, take the Line 2 (Blue) to Chernaya Rechka metro. From here, follow the riverbank north along Naberezhnaya Chernaya Rechka, turning right into Kolomyazhsky Prospect. After about 500m you'll see a track leading into the woods on your right: follow it.

Dostoevsky memorial at the 'Dom Raskolnikov'.

Dostoevsky's Near Execution

Alarmed at the revolutionary movements sweeping across Europe in 1848, Tsar Nicholas I's crackdown on dissident groups the following year included members of the Petrashevsky Circle (a group of intellectuals who met to discuss literature and Western philosophy banned by the Tsar). A plaque marks the spot (at **Vosnesensky Prospect d. 8**) where Dostoevsky was arrested in April 1849. He served several months in the **Secret House** of the Peter Paul Fortress (see p 66) before being led, with the other prisoners, to what is now **Pionerskaya Ploshad** (east of Vitebsky Vokzal, at the end of Gorokhovaya Ulitsa) to be executed on December 22nd. In what appears to have been a deliberate hoax (or torture) on the part of Nicholas I, they were reprieved only at the very last minute (when some had already been tied and blindfolded), and their sentences commuted to hard labor in Siberia. Dostoevsky was imprisoned again in 1874 for breaching censorship regulations as editor of *The Citizen* and detained for two days in the **Guard House** (now d. 37) at the north east corner of Sennaya Ploshad.

4 **Literaturnoye Kafe.** They'll promise you this was the last place Pushkin visited before the duel, but be careful: some of us remember when the Literaturnoye Café was a tiny one-room snack-spot on the other side of the canal. The steps they exhibit are authentic enough, however, and it's certainly true that the Wolf i Beranger café which once stood on this spot was a longstanding literary haunt. Lermontov's Death of a Poet was read aloud here days after the duel, and Dostoevsky's meeting with Petrashevsky here in 1846 was ultimately to lead to his imprisonment and near execution (see above). Take everything else with a bucket of salt, however, and be prepared for some shockingly rude service. *Nevsky Prospect d. 18.* ☎ *812 312 6057. $$.*

5 **The Alexander Pushkin Apartment Museum.** This was the impoverished Pushkin's last residence, from 1836–1837, and from which he went to his death. The key attraction is the poet's library, where his deathbed, deathmask, and a curl of hair in a locket are all on display. Be on your best behavior: the curators here have been trained in the finest traditions of pre-perestroika customer service, and allow access only with an audio guide (200R), strictly in groups, and only when they say so. *Nab. Reki Moiki d. 12.* ☎ *812 311 3531. www. museumpushkin.ru. Admission 100R adults, 80R kids. Wed–Mon 10.30am–5pm. Metro: Nevsky Prospect, Gostiny Dvor.*

6 ★★ **The Nabokov Museum.** Vladimir Nabokov (1899–1977, the Russian-born American author of *Lolita*) was born in this house, living here until his family's departure for the Crimea (and later England) in 1917. Everything you see is a recreation, the premises having been completely gutted after the Revolution. Curators have recreated the house as it would have appeared at the turn of the century when, thanks to Nabokov's father's position as head of the Constitutional Democratic Party and the St Petersburg Literary Fund, it was visited by luminaries including opera singer Fyodor Shalyapin, artist Alexander Benois and H.G. Wells. *B. Morskaya Ul. d. 47.* ☎ *812 315 4713. www.nabokovmuseum.org. Admission 100R. Tues–Fri 11am–6pm, Sat–Sun 12pm–5pm. Metro: Sadovaya, then bus 3, 22, 27 or marshrutka K169, K180, K190, K323.*

❼ ★★ Anna Akhmatova Museum in the Fontany Dom. It's somewhat incongruous to find a museum to one of the century's leading dissident poets in the Sheremetyev Palace, but this was Akhmatova's home in 1918, and

again from 1927–1952, converted into communal apartments (*communalki*) as so many buildings were after the Revolution. Many of her most important works were written here—or, more accurately, memorized to avoid confiscation by the authorities. With good reason: her first and third husbands were executed for 'anti-Stalinist' activities, and her son spent many years in the GULAG. Ask to hear a recording of Requiem (her most famous work, an indictment of life under Stalinism, not published in Russia until 1987) which includes extracts read by Akhmatova herself. Die-hard fans might also like to visit the Anna Akhmatova Museum of the Silver Age at Avtovskaya Ulitsa d. 12 (☎ 812 785 0442). *Liteiny Prospect d. 53.* ☎ *812 272 2211. www. akhmatova.spb.ru. Admission 200R. Tues–Sun 10.30am–6.30pm. Metro: Gostiny Dvor, Nevsky Prospect.*

The Akhmatova memorial in the Sheremetyev garden.

The People's War

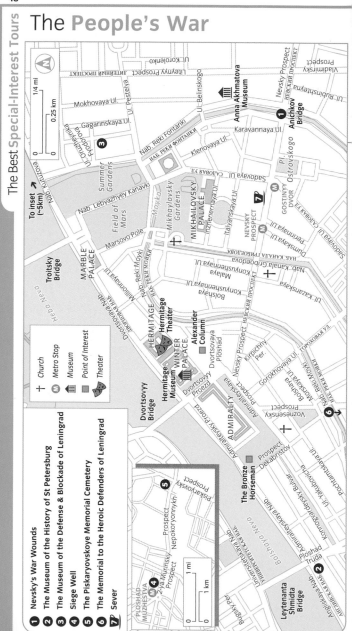

1 Nevsky's War Wounds
2 The Museum of the History of St Petersburg
3 The Museum of the Defense & Blockade of Leningrad
4 Siege Well
5 The Piskaryovskoye Memorial Cemetery
6 The Memorial to the Heroic Defenders of Leningrad
7 Sever

Legend:
+ Church
M Metro Stop
🏛 Museum
■ Point of Interest
🎭 Theater

Anna Akhmatova Museum
Anichkov Bridge
Nevsky Prospect
Vladimirsky Prospect
Rubinshteyna Ul.
Karavannaya Ul.
Mokhovaya Ul.
Gagarinskaya Ul.
Belinskogo Ul.
Klenovaya Ul.
Litevny Prospect ЛИТЕЙНЫЙ ПРОСПЕКТ
Ul. Korolenko
Ul. Pestelya
Nab. Reki Fontanki НАБ. РЕКИ ФОНТАНКИ
Sadovaya Ul. САДОВАЯ УЛ.
PL. Ostrovskogo
GOSTINY DVOR
NEVSKY PROSPECT
Dumskaya Ul.
Perinnaya Ul.
Inzhenernaya Ul.
Italianskaya Ul.
MIKHAILOVSKY PALACE
Mikhailovsky Gardens
Moyka
Summer Gardens
Field of Mars
Marsovo Pole
Nab. Lebyazhyey Kanavki
Troitsky Bridge
MARBLE PALACE
Dvortsovaya Nab.
Millionnaya Ul.
Nab. Reki Moyki НАБ. РЕКИ МОЙКИ
HERMITAGE
Hermitage Theater
Alexander Column
WINTER PALACE
Hermitage Museum
Dvortsovyy Proezd
Dvortsovaya Ploshad
Dvortsovy Bridge
ADMIRALTY
Admiralteysky Proezd
Admiralteyskaya
Prospect
Bolshaya Konyushennaya Ul.
Malaya Konyushennaya Ul.
Nab. kanala Griboedova НАБ. КАНАЛА ГРИБОЕДОВА
Ul. Kazanskaya
Gorokhovaya Ul.
Kirpichny Per.
Bolshaya Morskaya Ul.
Gorokhovaya Ul.
Voznesensky Prospect
Prospect Dekabristov
The Bronze Horseman
Ploshad Truda
Prospect Dekabristov
Pochtamtskaya Ul.
Ul. Yakubovicha
Konnogvardeysky Bulvar
Admiralteyskaya Nab.
Konnogvardeysky Nab.
BOLSHAYA NEVA БОЛЬШАЯ НЕВА
Universitetskaya Nab.
Leytenanta Shmidta Bridge
Angliyskaya Nab.
Bugsky Per.

Inset:
To inset (~5km)
1 mi
1 km
PLOSHAD MUZHESTVA
2-ya Murinsky Prospect
Piskaryovsky Prospect
Prospect Nepokoryonnykh

N
0 1/4 mi
0 0.25 km

To inset (~5km)

Almost 70 years on, the city still bears the marks of the 872 most difficult days of its history. Many of its pensioners still remember all too well the winter of 1942 when, without power, heating, or water the population subsisted on a ration of 125 grams of bread per person per day. If you're here on May 9th (Victory Day) or January 27th (the final day of the Siege) you'll see them, marching with old comrades on Palace Square or remembering loved ones in the Piskaryovskoye and Serafimovskoye cemeteries. **START: from Nevsky Prospect metro towards the Anichkov Bridge.**

❶ ★★ **Nevsky's War Wounds.** The city's main thoroughfare still bears the scars of the Siege. The shell damage on the granite base of the Anichkov Bridge has never been repaired, a small plaque remarking on the other 148, 478 shellings endured. Further south, No. 54/3 (on the corner of Malaya Sadovaya Ulitsa) still carries the transmitter used to broadcast news during the darkest days. Most poignant of all, the former School 210 at No. 14 still bears a plaque warning 'Citizens, during bombardment it is safer on the other side of the street!'

❷ **The Museum of the History of St Petersburg.** From the early shelter-building of September 1941 through the starvation and cold of the murderous winter of 1941–1942 to the valiant clean-up efforts of spring 1942, this is a painstaking rec-reation of the days of war. Don't miss Tanya Slmacheva's childhood diary in Room 18, or the chaotic photos of the evacuations via Lake Ladoga (Room 20). Given the extent to which historical records have obliterated Stalin's role in the war, the appear-ance of that profile alongside Lenin's on union banners in Room 21 is something of a shock. *Angliiskaya Nab. d. 44.* ☎ *812 571 7544. Admission 100R adults, 60R kids. Metro: Nevsky Prospect, then bus 22.*

❸ ★ **The Museum of the Defense & Blockade of Lenin-grad.** A frustrating experience without

The Rumyantsev mansion, home to the Museum of the History of St. Petersburg.

an interpreter. A stellar collection of wartime propaganda posters would be much improved with some translation and the most fascinating exhibits (including examples of German and Finnish propaganda distributed by air-drop) will be lost on non-speakers. Nonetheless, the recreation of a Siege-time apartment—with only the beat of a metronome broadcast to indicate the radio station was not yet under attack—is an evocative recreation of the childhoods endured by today's pensioners. *Solyarny Per. d. 9.* ☎ *812 275 7208. Admission 150R adults, 40R kids. Metro: Chernishevskaya.*

The Siege of Leningrad

While the entire population had been conscripted to help build defenses months earlier, September 8, 1941 saw the city almost completely encircled by German and Finnish forces and the 872-day siege began. The city's pre-war population of 3 million was decimated: some 1.5 million soldiers and civilians dying of wounds, starvation, and cold, and an almost equal number evacuated across the Road of Life—the only route out of the city across the frozen ice of Lake Ladoga during the winters of 1941–1943. More than half a million people crossed it during that first winter, when the ice held from November 21st, 1941 to April 24th, 1942. Conditions were eased in January 1943 when the Red Army overcame German forces south of Lake Ladoga to establish a land corridor, but the city remained under attack until January 27th, 1944. It was awarded the status of Heroic City (the first in the USSR) a year later.

4 Siege Well. Resist the impulse to jump straight onto a marshrutka for the Piskarevskoye Cemetery. Instead, bear left out of the metro onto Prospect Nepokoryonnikh, to find a small memorial on your left at No. 6. The inscription reads: 'Here, during the gruelling years of the Blockade, stood a life-giving well.' No understatement: as all archive footage of the Siege (see below) makes explicitly clear. *Prospect*

The Piskaryovskoye Memorial Cemetery.

Nepokoryonnikh d. 6. Metro: Ploshad Muzhestva.

5 The Piskaryovskoye Memorial Cemetery. It's located in one of the city's most depressing suburbs, but this cemetery, containing an estimated half million military and civilian victims, is testament to the appalling human cost of the Siege. While the cemetery was pressed into use from 1941–1944, this memorial complex was not opened until 1960. The vast majority of graves, you'll notice, are marked 1941 and 1942: victims of that first awful winter. *Prospect Nepokoryonnikh d. 74. ☎ 812 247 5716. Admission free. 10am–6pm (to 9pm summer). Metro: Ploshad Muzhestva, then bus 138 or 178.*

6 The Memorial to the Heroic Defenders of Leningrad. Opened on May 9th, 1975 (the 30th anniversary of the end of WWII), this is the most striking (and certainly the most graphic) of the many memorials in the city: its architects (V. A, Kamensky, S. B. Speransky, and M. K. Anikushin) having themselves all participated in the Blockade. The bronze

The Memorial to the Heroic Defenders of Leningrad.

figures on either side of the 48-meter high granite obelisk face the southernmost extent of the Blockade front line, at the Pulkovo Heights. The Memorial Hall directly below (opened February 1978) has no information in English, but a bronze relief map in the center of the hall shows the extent of the Blockade and the movements of the German forces. Curators will go out of their way to show you the most poignant exhibits, including the daily bread ration. But the most striking feature, however, is the archive footage shot during the Siege: of corpses left on the street or towed on sledges, and women scooping water from beneath the ice on the frozen canals. *Ploshad Pobedy.* ☎ *812 371 2951. Admission 50R. 10am–6pm (to 5pm Tues and Fri). Closed Wed and last Tues of every month. Metro: Moskovskaya, then bus 3, 11, 39, 55 or trolleybus 27, 29, 45.*

7 Sever. Still standing after Revolution, two World Wars and the 872-day Siege. *See p 96. Nevsky Prospect d. 44.* ☎ *812 571 2589. Metro: Nevsky Prospect. Map p 48. $.*

A Walk Along the Frontline

Or, more prosaically, a marshrutka ride. The Memorial to the Heroic Defenders of Leningrad marks the southernmost extent of the Blockade (and the scene of some of the most severe fighting), at the Pulkovo Heights. From the Memorial, take any bus to Moskovskaya metro, where you will find a WWII bunker (or **DOT**) outside the northernmost wing of the **Dom Sovetov (a)**, since preserved as part of the **Green Belt of Glory**: a 200-kilometer route of former bunkers marking the outer limits of the city's defenses. Buses 26, 114, 130 and numerous marshrutki (K29, K43, K45, K49, K339, K114, K130) will get you to **Leninsky Prospect d. 136 (b)**, where you'll find another. From here, the K344 marshrutka will take you to the top of the junction with Tramvainy Prospect. Head west then north along Prospect Stachek to No. 91 where, on the other side of the street, you will find the **Kirovsky Zavod KV-85 Memorial (c)** and the **Memorial Tram (d)**.

Famous **Residents**

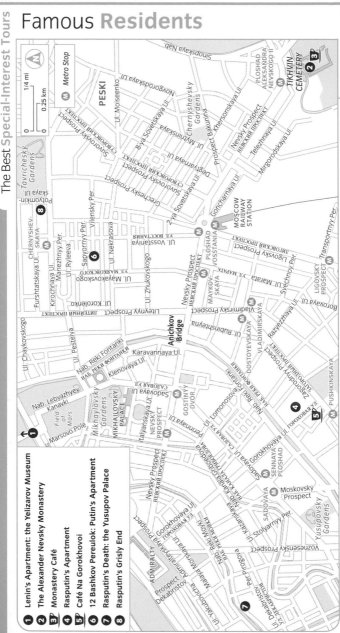

1. Lenin's Apartment: the Yelizarov Museum
2. The Alexander Nevsky Monastery
3. Monastery Café
4. Rasputin's Apartment
5. Café Na Gorokhovoi
6. 12 Bashkov Pereulok: Putin's Apartment
7. Rasputin's Death: the Yusupov Palace
8. Rasputin's Grisly End

While not the most glamorous tour, this route does allow you to uncover the often inauspicious beginnings of the country's greatest heroes (or villains), from the extended families of Lenin and Stalin, to the grisly and protracted death of Rasputin and the pre-presidential formative years of Vladimir Putin. START: **at Chkalovskaya metro, heading west for the Yelizarov museum on Ulitsa Lenina.**

❶ ★★★ Lenin's Apartment: the Yelizarov Museum. With not a single hammer or sickle in sight, this museum is a flawless recreation of pre-revolutionary intelligentsia life. Belonging to Mark Yelizarov, husband of Lenin's elder sister Anna, this apartment in the 1912 'Boat House' was a typical *dohodny dom* (an apartment building developed for rental) of the time. Lenin lived here only from April–July 1917 (in a cramped room containing his and Nadezhda's two single beds), but the many photos and memorabilia (all of them genuine) give a real sense of the private life of the Ulyanovs. *Ul. Lenina d. 52 apt. 24 (press '24' on the intercom for entry).* ☎ *812 325 3778.*

Admission 200R. 10am–6pm closed Wed and Sun. Metro: Chkalovskaya.

❷ ★★★ The Alexander Nevsky Monastery. Take a minute to explore the remaining five churches of this monastery (founded by Peter I in 1710), and don't ignore the Lazarev Cemetery on your left: it holds the graves of the great city architects Quarenghi and Rossi, as well as Pushkin's wife Natalia Goncharova. The Tikhvin Cemetery opposite is the real must-see, however. If you enjoy this, you might also like to visit Lenin's mother and sisters, as well as writers Ivan Turgenev and Alexander Blok, in the **Volkovskoye Cemetery** (Rasstanaya Ul. d. 30. ☎ 812 766 2383).

The Alexander Nevsky Monastery.

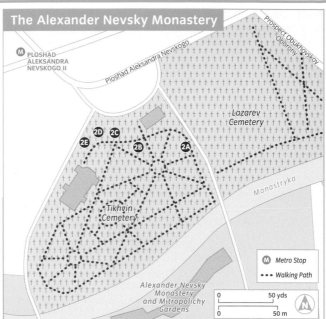

The Alexander Nevsky Monastery

M PLOSHAD
ALEKSANDRA
NEVSKOGO II

Prospect Obukhovskoy Oborony

Ploshad Aleksandra Nevskogo

Lazarev
Cemetery

2D 2C
2E
2B
2A

Monastryka

Tikhvin
Cemetery

M Metro Stop
• • • Walking Path

Alexander Nevsky
Monastery
and Mitropolichy
Gardens

| 0 | 50 yds |
| 0 | 50 m |

2A Fyodor Dostoevsky (1821-1881) Достоевский Федор Михайлович (1821-1881)

2B Mikhail Glinka (1804-1857) Глинка Михаий Иванович (1804-1857)

2C Nikolai Rismky-Korsakoff (1844-1908) Римского-Корсаков Никопач (1844-1908)

2D Modest Mussorgsky (1839-1881) Мусоргский (1839-1881) Модест Петрович

2E Pyotr Tchaikovsky (1840-1893) Чайковский Петр Ильич (1840-1893)

Ploshad Alexandra Nevskovo d. 1. Monastery 6am–10pm, the Trinity Cathedral 6am–8pm. Admission 100R adults, 50R kids. Lazarev Monastery 9.30am–6pm. Admission 160R adults, 80R kids. Tikhvin Monastery ☎ 812 717 1716. 9.30am–7.30pm (variable). Admission 100R adults, 50R kids.

3 Monastery Café. Steamy, crowded, and very reminiscent of pre-perestroika catering, this tiny café is recommended, nonetheless, for its fabulous views across the monastery courtyard. *Ploshad Alexandra Nevskovo d. 1. No phone. $.*

4 Rasputin's Apartment. It was from this grim and potholed courtyard that Felix Yusupov led the blissfully ignorant Rasputin to his death on the night of December 16th 17th 1916. Still a residential address, you won't be able to see the inside of apartment No. 20 (on the second floor of the block on your right as you enter the courtyard), but the building is appropriately Gothic. If you'd like to relive Rasputin's last days, Go Petersburg rent several apartments within the building, from €70 per night. *Gorokhovaya Ul. d. 64, apt. 20. Metro: Pushkinskaya. Go Petersburg* ☎ *8 921 745 4269. www. gopetersburg.spb.ru.*

5 Café Na Gorokhovoi. Directly opposite Rasputin's apartment, this elegant bistro offers traditional Russian zakuski (snacks) and a reasonably priced cup of coffee. *Ul. Gorokhovaya d. 73.* ☎ *812 713 5779. $.*

6 12 Bashkov Pereulok: Putin's Apartment. It would be tempting to assume that the super-pristine façade on this building has been refurbished in honor of its illustrious former resident, but no. Go through the courtyard and hope that the door directly opposite you is open. If it is, go straight up to the second floor: the apartment on the left is where the young Vladimir Vladimirovich lived his misspent youth, before signing up to the KGB in 1975. No lighting, peeling paintwork, and a worryingly loose banister. Just one of the people, really. *Baskov Per. d. 12. Metro: Chernishevskaya.*

7 ★★ Rasputin's Death: the Yusupov Palace. The circumstances of Rasputin's death have become the stuff of legend: refusing to die after cyanide-laced cakes, shots at close range, and a beating with an iron bar, he was finally dumped into the Malaya Nevka near Krestovsky Island (see p 106), where he died of hypothermia. Guided tours of the basement dining room (complete with wax figures recreating the fateful tea party) are only available at 1.45pm daily, and only in Russian (although English-language tours can be

arranged). Far better, in my view, to concentrate on the interior, of one of the few aristocratic palaces remaining in its original (albeit reconstructed) state. Don't miss the private theater, the Moorish Room, or the Mauritanian Parlour. *Nab. Reki Moiki d. 94.* ☎ *812 332 1991. www.yusupov-palace.ru. Admission 450R, adults, 350R students, 250R kids. 11am–5pm daily. Metro: Sennaya Ploshad, Sadovaya.*

8 Rasputin's Grisly End. Allegedly castrated after his murder, Rasputin's penis was, apparently, returned to his daughter Maria in 1977 and put up for auction at Bonhams in 1994: although that exhibit was later found to be a sea cucumber. Clinic director Igor Knyazkin claims to have bought this item from a French collector, together with several hand-written letters. Be warned though: 28.5 cm of the mad monk's man muscle might be a bit much for the faint hearted, not to mention the other exhibits in this museum, located within a urology clinic. *Furshtatskaya Ul. d. 47/11.* ☎ *812 320 7600. Admission 100R. 9am–8pm daily. Metro: Chernishevskaya.*

The Yusupov Palace.

Outlandish Architecture

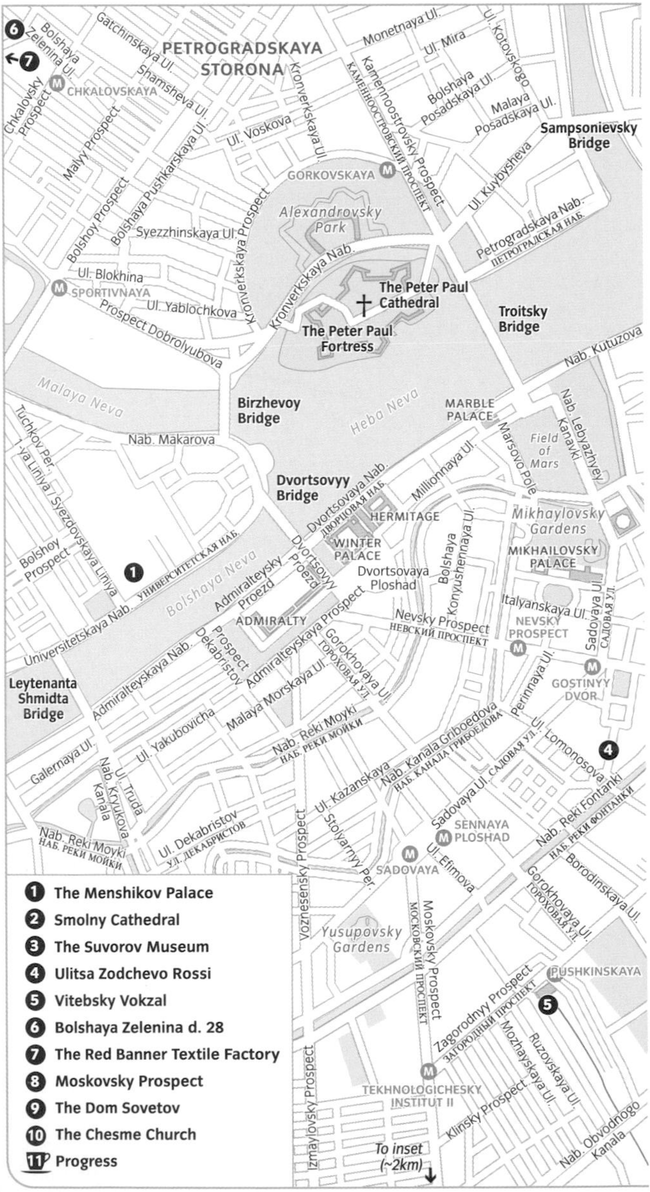

1 The Menshikov Palace
2 Smolny Cathedral
3 The Suvorov Museum
4 Ulitsa Zodchevo Rossi
5 Vitebsky Vokzal
6 Bolshaya Zelenina d. 28
7 The Red Banner Textile Factory
8 Moskovsky Prospect
9 The Dom Sovetov
10 The Chesme Church
11 Progress

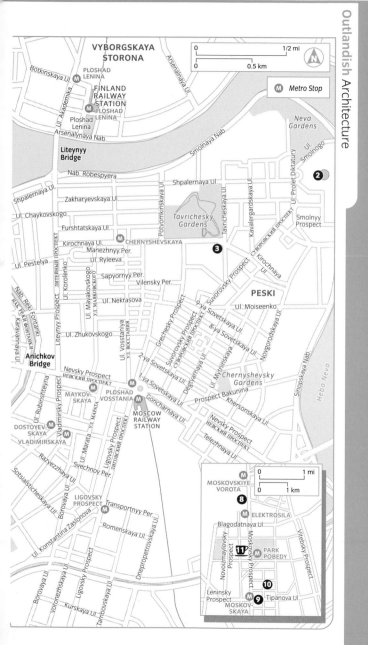

St Petersburg's architectural history can be traced quite simply, from the early Baroque of Peter's new city, through the Neoclassicism of Catherine the Great on Nevsky Prospect and Palace Square, to the Stalinist Classicism of the dictator's failed attempt to re-create a new city center along Moskovsky Prospect. Some of the most startling examples, however, are off the beaten track. This tour will take you, in chronological order, through the best of them.
START: at Vasileostrovskaya metro, heading south through the 7th Line for the Menshikov Palace.

① ★★ The Menshikov Palace.
The heart of Peter the Great's new city is easily identified in Domenico Trezzini's Venetian grid-like layout of Vasilievsky Island, and his Petrine Baroque buildings that line the Neva: the Peter Paul Cathedral (originally built in 1712–1733), and the Twelve Colleges (1722–1744). The most striking example of Petrine Baroque, of course, is Trezzini's Summer Palace (1710–1714, see p 18), but this palace, built for the city's first Governor and one-time favorite Alexander Danilovich Menshikov is a far grander affair. See p 80 for the full tour.

② ★★★ Smolny Cathedral.
Petrine Baroque was to become far

The Smolny Cathedral.

more rococo under Peter's daughter Empress Elizabeth: her architect of choice, Francesco Bartolomeo Rastrelli being responsible for rebuilding the Winter Palace (1754–1762, see p 31), as well as the palaces at Peterhof (1745–1753, see p 160) and Tsarskoye Selo (1752, see p 156). Construction was begun by Rastrelli 1748–1764, although it was not completed until 1835. After Rastrelli was dismissed by Catherine the Great in 1762, Yuri Felten was appointed to complete the project, building a 'School for Noble Girls' and separate establishment for 'Lower Middle Class Girls', in 1764. I always think it's best viewed from a distance, its rococo excess contrasting sharply with the Constructivism of the **Bolshoi Dom** (the FSB headquarters) just up the road at Liteiny Prospect d. 4 (see p 69). *Ploshad Rastrelli d. 3/1.* ☎ *812 577 1278. www.eng.cathedral.ru/smolny. Admission 100R. Daily 10am–8pm, closed Wed. Metro: Chernishevskaya, then bus 22, 46, 136, 105.*

③ ★★★ The Suvorov Museum.
Chronologically, this Russian Revival building should follow the Neoclassicism of Ul. Zodchevo Rossi. But the convenience of a K15 marshrutka ride direct from Smolny can't be ignored. Dedicated to Russia's last Generalissimo, Alexander Suvorov, it was built in 1904 in the Russian Revival style (an idealized form of 'folk' architecture popular in the latter half of the 19th century), by A.I.

The Russian Revival Suvorov Museum.

van Gogen and G.D. Grimm. The two massive mosaics on the outer walls show Suvorov leaving to fight the French Revolutionary armies in Italy, and his march across the Alps. According to the *Encyclopedia of St Petersburg* (www.encspb.ru) this area was, in the mid-19th century, a cheap red-light district: fees apparently ranging from 30 kopeks to one

The Style Moderne Vitebsky Vokzal.

ruble. *43 Kirochnaya Ul.* ☎ *812 579 3914. Admission 250R adults, 150R kids. Daily 10am–6pm, closed Tues–Wed.*

④ Ulitsa Zodchevo Rossi. The city was transformed again on Catherine the Great's accession in 1762, the results still evident in the Neoclassical buildings lining Nevsky Prospect and Palace Square: the Russian National Library (Yegor Sokolov, 1796–1801) Gostiny Dvor (completed by Jean-Baptiste Vallin de la Mothe after Bartolomeo Rastrelli's more extravagant 1757 design was rejected), Giacomo Quarenghi's Hermitage Theater (1783–1787) and Carlo Rossi's General Staff Building (1819–1829). My personal favorite, however, is this street leading off from Ostrovskaya Ploshad. Tiny and perfectly formed (its 22-meter width the same height as the buildings on either side) it was completed by its namesake in 1832.

⑤ ★★★ Vitebsky Vokzal. Russia's first station opened in 1837, with a somewhat limited route running only as far as the royal estate of Tsarskoye Selo. Rebuilt in its

Pristine Style Moderne mosaics at Bolshaya Zelenina d.28.

entirety in 1901–1904, impressive as Stanislaw Brzozowski's building is, Sima Minash's stunning 1904 Style Moderne interior is second only to the Grand Hotel Europe (see p 150) for sheer opulence. Bear right (past the original molded benches) to the main hall, but don't miss the equally ornate ticket office on the second floor. Before getting back on the metro, take a minute to walk west to the fire station at **Zagorodny Prospect d. 56**: a perfect piece of Constructivism, built in 1931–1934. Play your cards right and the super-friendly crew might let you tour the interior, and show you bomb damage sustained on the tower during the Siege. *Zagorodny Prospect d. 52.* ☎ 812 768 5807.

⑥ ★★★ Bolshaya Zelenina d. 28. This rental apartment building was built in 1904–1905 for the head of the noble family of Leuchtenberg. He didn't get to enjoy his investment for long, becoming a White Russian émigré immediately after the Revolution. Artist S.T. Shelkovo's five panels depict moored vessels, pastoral scenes, and an

industrial landscape. Try to get into the *dvor* (courtyard) if you can: it's just as good on the inside.

⑦ ★★★ The Red Banner Textile Factory. Retrace your steps along B. Zelenina, turning right into Korpusnaya Ulitsa: the avant garde outline of this building on the corner of Pionerskaya will be visible as you approach. The 'Expressionist' architect Erich Mendelsohn was the first foreign architect invited to the Soviet Union to design this building in 1926: its ship-like design marking a very clear difference with purist Russian Constructivism (see below). Political instability (or, some claim, lack of materials) meant only the central power station (facing you) was constructed as he had intended, and the project was finally completed by Russian architects led by Hyppolit Petreaus in 1937. Now in a state of some dereliction, plans were announced in summer 2008 for its re-development as a retail, residential, and office complex. Don't miss the white memorial directly in front, dedicated to the country's first Pioneer Brigade, formed here in 1923. *Pionerskaya Ul. d. 57. Metro: Chkalovskaya.*

⑧ ★★ Moskovsky Prospect. The center of Stalin's 1935 planned relocation of the city center, the southernmost section of Moskovsky Prospect is, inevitably, dominated by Stalinist Classicism. The more northern section, however, around Moskovskiye Vorota metro has some of the country's most noteworthy Constructivist buildings. The former 1931 **Kapranov *Dvorets Kultury* (Palace of Culture)** at No. 97 is rapidly being subsumed into a massive retail-business complex (rumored to include a new Intercontinental Hotel), due to open in 2009. The façade has been retained, however, identifiable by the two smaller buildings at the front. The former **Ilyich DK** at No. 152 (1930–1931) still functions as the 'Moskovsky Cultural-Relaxation Center.' The must-see building on this stretch, however, is the **District Soviet** at No. 129, built from 1930–1935 by a team including the leading post-Constructivist architect Ivan Fomin.

⑨ ★★ The Dom Sovetov. So called only from 1956 onwards (it had been Prospect im. Stalina since December 1950), the city's longest street bears the unmistakeable mark of the dictator's iron hand, dominated by the (very Muscovite) Stalinist Classicism that prevailed until his death in 1956. The centerpiece, the Dom Sovetov at No. 212, was built by Noi Trotsky, 1936–1941. The statue of Lenin in front was erected in 1970, on the 100th anniversary of his birth. *Moskovsky Prospect d. 129.*

⑩ ★★★ The Chesme Church. Somewhat out of chronological order, this building is simply too surreal to put anywhere else—a pink and white Gothic extravaganza built by Yuri Velten in 1780 for Catherine the Great, commemorating the 1770 victory over the Turks at Chesme Bay. You may be told that this church was previously used as a GULAG. Not quite true: a forced labor camp was in fact housed (from 1919–1924) in a wing of the Chesma Palace. You will see it across Ul. Lensoveta if you stand with the church behind you. *Chesma Palace, Ul Gastello d. 15. Chesma Church, Ul. Lensoveta d. 12. ☎ 812 443 6114. Daily 9am–7pm. Metro: Moskovskaya.*

⑪ Progress. You'll find numerous snack spots on Moskovsky Prospect. My favorite is this retro-Soviet cake shop opposite Park Pobedy. *Moskovsky Prospect d. 168. ☎ 812 388 1547. $.*

Yuri Velten's 1780 Chesme Church.

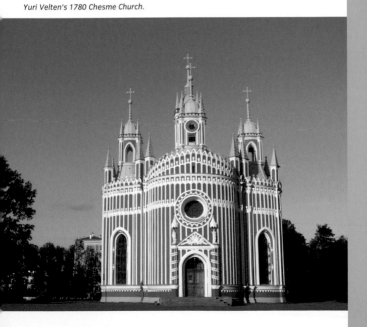

The Peter Paul **Fortress**

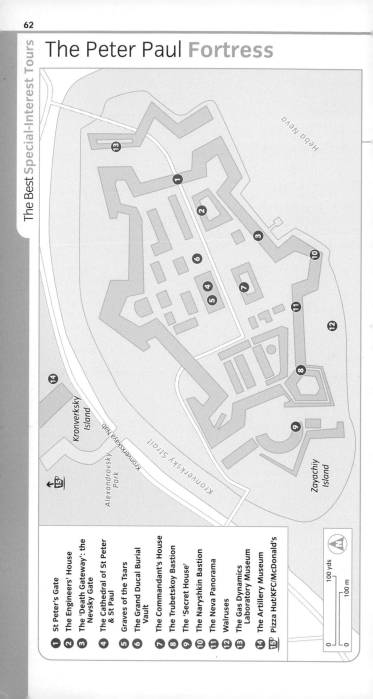

1 St Peter's Gate
2 The Engineers' House
3 The 'Death Gateway': the Nevsky Gate
4 The Cathedral of St Peter & St Paul
5 Graves of the Tsars
6 The Grand Ducal Burial Vault
7 The Commandant's House
8 The Trubetskoy Bastion
9 The 'Secret House'
10 The Naryshkin Bastion
11 The Neva Panorama
12 Walruses
13 The Gas Dynamics Laboratory Museum
14 The Artillery Museum
15 Pizza Hut/KFC/McDonald's

Heвa Neva

Kronverksky Island

Alexandrovsky Park

Kronverkskaya Nab.

Kronverksky Strait

Zayachiy Island

100 yds

100 m

0
0

The foundation of Peter the Great's new city, and the final resting place of the Romanov Tsars, on a summer day (or even a crisp winter one) this is probably one of the most child-friendly attractions in town, with guns, dungeons, a beach, and some secret tunnels. **START: from Petrogradskaya metro (or, if it has re-opened, Gorkhovskaya), heading south down Kamennostrovsky Prospect and over the Ioannovsky Bridge to St Peter's Gate.**

The Peter Paul Fortress.

1 **St Peter's Gate.** Founded on May 16th 1703 (May 27th under the Julian calendar, now commemorated as City Day), the Peter Paul Fortress was built at some speed under the direction of Peter I and the various nobles from whom its six bastions take their names (Gosudarev, Naryshkin, Trubetskoy, Zotov, Golovkin and Menshikov). While keeping the Russian tradition of a fortified kremlin, the Dutch and Italian influences of the Petrine Baroque architecture here are quite clear: the angular layout of the complex, in particular, a direct imitation of Italian fortresses. This gate (originally built in 1708, and later rebuilt in 1716–1717 under Domenico Trezzini) is likely to be the first you will see if

arriving on foot from Gorkhovskaya metro, and the symbolism is telling: as well as the Romanov eagle, a relief of St Peter casting down Simon is an allegory of Peter the Great's victory over Charles XII of Sweden in the Great Northern War of 1700–1721. A note for parents: kids will love the tanks at the Artillery Museum, directly behind the fortress across the Kronverksky Canal. But you'll need to visit Thursday to Sunday if you want to cover both in one day. *The Peter Paul Fortress, Hare Island.* ☎ *812 230 6431. Single ticket to all areas excl. the cathedral, 250R adults, 130R students. Individual museums 100R adults, 60R students (including schoolchildren).Unless otherwise shown, museums and exhibitions are open daily 11am–6pm (to 5pm Tues), closed Wed. Fortress grounds open daily 6am–10pm. Metro: Gorkhovskaya.*

City Day celebrations at the Fortress.

Mikhail Shemiakin's controversial Peter the Great.

❷ The Engineers' House. Buillt in 1748–1749, the young Dostoevsky worked here on graduating from the military academy in the Engineers' Castle. Directly behind you will find Mikhail Shemiakin's controversial 1991 statue of Peter the Great: less than heroic, but said to be an almost exact reproduction of his height and size.

❸ The 'Death Gateway': the Nevsky Gate. It's through this gate that prisoners would be led to their executions, typically at the Schlisselberg Fortress, some 50 miles east on the coast of Lake Ladoga. Plaques on the underside of its arch show high-water marks of the city's most serious floods: reaching 12ft 10 inches above normal water level on November 7th, 1824.

❹ ★★ The Cathedral of St Peter & St Paul. The foundations for Domenico Trezzini's original cathedral were laid in 1712, and it was consecrated in 1733. It was completely rebuilt (after a series of fires) in 1776. Converted into a museum in 1924, services resumed in 2000. Legend has it that restorers in 1997 uncovered a note (secreted in the angel weathervane on the top of the tower) left by Soviet craftsmen, apologizing for the condition of the materials and the work: they, in turn, left a note for future generations. *Admission 170R adults, 80R students. Belltower 100R, 60R students.10am–6pm (to 5pm Tues), closed Wed.*

❺ Graves of the Tsars. All of the Romanov Tsars and Tsarinas are here, with the exception of Peter II (buried in the Kremlin's Archangel Cathedral) and Ivan VI (buried in Schlisselberg).

The Cathedral of St Peter & St Paul.

Graves of the Tsars

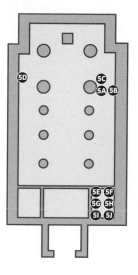

5A Peter the Great (1672-1725) Tsar | Пётр | Апексеевич (1672-1725), император

5B Catherine I (1684-1727) Tsarina (Empress) Екатерина I Апексеевна (1684-1727), императрича

5C Catherine the Great (1729-1796) Tsarina (Empress) Екатерина II Апексеевна (1729-1796), императрича

5D Paul I (1754-1801) Tsar Павеп I Петрович (1754-1801), император

5E Nicholas II (18268-1918) Tsar Никопай II Александрович (1868-1918), император

5F Alexandra Romanova (1872-1918) Tsarina Апександра Фёдоровна (1872-1918), императрича

5G Grand Duchess Olga Romanova (1895-1918) Опьга Никопаевна (1895-1918), великая княжна

5H Grand Duchess Tatiana Romanova (1897-19198) Татьяна (1897-1918), великая княжна

5I Grand Duchess Anastasia Romanova (1901-1918) Анастасия Никопаевна (1901-1918), великая княжна

5J Tsarevitch Alexei Romanov (1904-1918) Апексей Никопаевич (1904-1918), великий князь

6 The Grand Ducal Burial Vault. Built at the end of the 19th century for more distant royal relatives as the cathedral reached capacity. Perhaps more interesting is the exhibition on the History of the Mint, containing, among other items, coins featuring the profile of Stalin.

7 The Commandant's House. Originally built in 1743–1746, but significantly amended in the late 19th century, it was here that participants in the 1826 Decembrist Uprising and members of the Petrashevsky Circle (including Dostoevsky in 1849) were tried. It was again pressed into use in October 1917, as the headquarters for an armed uprising against the Provisional Government, under the direction of the Petrograd Military-Revolutionary Committee: ultimately leading to the attack on the Winter Palace. It now hosts an exhibition on the pre-revolutionary history of St Petersburg. Scan the *St Petersburg Times* for details of occasional concerts here. ☎ 812 243 3484.

8 The Trubetskoy Bastion. The Fortress has a gruesome history of incarcerating opponents to the Tsars, beginning with the

Winter day at the Nevsky Gate.

imprisonment (and ultimate murder) of Peter the Great's own son, Alexei, in 1718. The Trubetskoy Bastion was built in 1870–1872. The anarchist Pyotr Kropotkin was later held here, as was one Alexander Ulyanov, brother of Lenin, arrested for his involvement in an attempted assassination of Alexander III. It was Alexander's execution in 1887 at the age of 21 that galvanized his brother into a life of political activity. Maxim Gorky and Leon Trotsky both served time here in 1905. Members of the Provisional Government, arrested during the events of October 26th were imprisoned here in 1917, as were opponents of the Bolsheviks in 1918–1919. *10am–6pm (to 5pm Tues), closed Wed.*

9 The 'Secret House'. While an early wooden prison was built here as early as 1768, it was the 'Secret House' which cast terror into the souls of the early inhabitants: a single-storey stone house built in 1797, intended to hold 20 prisoners in solitary confinement. Sample cells in the Zotov bastion give a good idea of the Spartan conditions they endured. The same building later held members of the Decembrists, and in 1849 members of the Petrashevsky Circle, including Fyodor Dostoevsky. The Secret House was demolished in 1893, and the Ministry of War Archives erected in its place. It now houses administrators of the Museum of St Petersburg.

10 kids The Naryshkin Bastion. Originally initiated by Peter the Great, the tradition of firing the midday cannon here was revived by Brezhnev for the city's 250th anniversary celebrations in 1957. Don't be confused: the 250th anniversary celebrations (due 1953) were postponed for four years due to Stalin's untimely demise that year.

The Artillery Museum.

⓫ kids The Neva Panorama.
Perfect exercise for hyperactive kids on a good day, but a miserable wind-chilling mud-squelching trek on a bad one. It's best approached from the Secret Passage of the Gosudarev Bastion: don't miss the Rolls-Royce Silver Ghost just as you emerge. *11am–7pm (to 6pm 1st Nov to 28th Feb.)*

⓬ Walruses. Not the long-toothed kind, but those brave and eccentric souls who break the mid-winter ice on the beach next to the Naryshkin Bastion for a quick dip (and, doubtless, a few shots). It's a popular sunbathing spot in summer, and scene of the annual Sand Sculpture festival.

⓭ kids The Gas Dynamics Laboratory Museum. Early rocket science. Originally established in Moscow in 1921, the I. Tikhomirov Laboratory for the Development of Inventions was moved to St Petersburg in 1925 to begin work on rocket projectiles. Renamed the Gas Dynamic Laboratory that year, it began work with the Moscow Rocket Research Institute in 1933. Exhibits include full-scale models of early rockets, and the Soyuz 16 descent capsule.

⓮ kids The Artillery Museum. Covering more than 15,000 square meters, with pieces dating from the original 'Memorial Hall' artillery collection of 1756, this might be a bit much for all but the most hardened battle fans. The outdoor heavy artillery collection, however, is a must for males of all ages. *Alexandrovsky Park d. 7. ☎ 812 232 0296, ☎ 812 232 0704. Wed–Sun 11am–6pm.*

⓯ Pizza Hut/KFC/McDonald's. You'll find various snack stops inside the fortress, but if you're taking young ones you might want to make sure they're fed first. You'll find Pizza Hut, KFC/Rostiks and McDonald's beside the Petrogradskaya metro, one stop (or a No.46 bus ride) away. *Petrogradskaya metro. $.*

Prisons & Prisoners

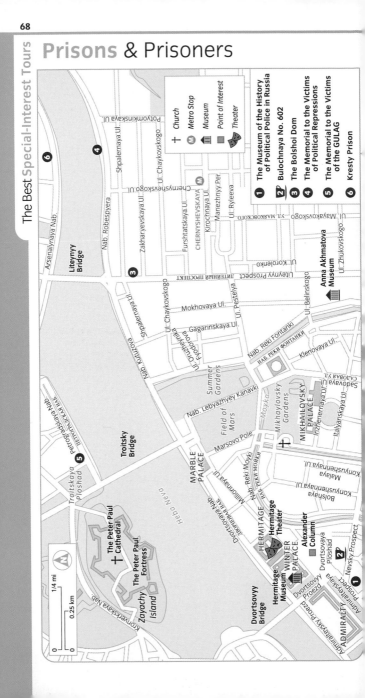

- ✝ Church
- Ⓜ Metro Stop
- 🏛 Museum
- ▪ Point of Interest
- 🎭 Theater

1 The Museum of the History of Political Police in Russia
2 Bulochnaya No. 602
3 The Bolshoi Dom
4 The Memorial to the Victims of Political Repressions
5 The Memorial to the Victims of the GULAG
6 Kresty Prison

At a time when much Russian tourism seems to descend into communist pastiche and Soviet kitsch, it's worth having a look at some of the sights you won't find in the City Government's Official Guide. A tour of this kind could, without due respect to each site's many victims, cross the fine line between historical interest and voyeurism: on balance, however, the less edifying aspects of the city's Soviet history are too important to ignore. START: **at the former memorial museum of Felix Dzerzhinsky, founder of the KGB.**

❶ The Museum of the History of Political Police in Russia.

This building was, until 1975, a memorial museum to Felix Dzerzhinsky, founder of the Cheka, the early forerunner to the KGB, and the key attraction for non-Russian speakers is likely to be his former office where, as Chairman of the All-Russia Special Commission for Counter Revolution and Sabotage, he interrogated numerous young radicals, including Lenin. Exhibitions on the secret services from 1920–1990, and 'The KGB in the USSR' hold considerable declassified material, but this may well prove to be a frustrating experience without an interpreter. *Admiralteisky Prospect. D. 6.* ☎ *812 312 2742,* ☎ *812 312 6305. Admission 200R. Mon–Fri 10am–6pm.*

❷ **Bulochnaya No. 602.** An appropriately old-school cake and coffee stop at the bottom of Nevsky Prospect. *Nevsky Prospect d. 6.* ☎ *812 312 6084. $.*

❸ The Bolshoi Dom. Take no

photos: this building (built in 1931–1932 on the site of the former District Court, burnt down by protesters during the Revolution of 1917) remains a 'protected object' and your camera will be confiscated if you are caught. Architecturally interesting, marking the transition from Constructivism to the later Soviet Classicism, the *Bolshoi Dom* (Big House) remains notorious as a St Petersburg branch of the Federal

Memorial to the Victims of the GULAG.

The Kresty Prison.

Security Service (FSB): the post-perestroika re-incarnation of the KGB. It connects directly to **Shpalernaya Ul. d. 25,** now a remand prison but known until 1917 as the House of Preliminary Detention, used to hold members of revolutionary movements, including Lenin (in cell 193) from 1895–1897. **No. 38 Shpalernaya** is also worth a look: only a tiny plaque on the front indicates that this is a branch of the FSB. But the statue of Cheka (KGB) founder Felix Dzerzhinsky at the front is a bit of a giveaway. *Liteiny Prospect d. 4. No access. Metro: Chernishevskaya.*

❹ ★ The Memorial to the Victims of Political Repressions. Viewed from one angle this memorial appears to be a typical statue of two sphinxes. Viewed from the other side, however—facing the Kresty Prison (below)—the sphinxes' exposed skeletons make clear the anger of sculptor Mikhail Shemyakin, a former exile, repeatedly incarcerated in mental hospitals and

expelled from the Academy of Arts in 1971. The base includes extracts and quotations from the country's most famous dissidents, including Solzhenitsyn, Mandelstam, and Akhmatova. *Nab. Robispierre, between nos 12–14. Metro: Chernishevskaya.*

❺ ★★ The Memorial to the Victims of the GULAG. This austere stone slab, adorned only with a strand of barbed wire, was erected in 2002. The stone is from the Solovetsky Special Designation Camp, opened in the early days of the Revolution on an island in the White Sea, one of the first labor camps from which the GULAG system was to evolve. Directly behind it stands a classic piece of Constructivist architecture, the House of Political Convicts. *Troitskaya Ploshad d. 1. Metro: Gorkhovskaya.*

❻ Kresty Prison. Originally a wine warehouse, this complex was converted to prison accommodation following the liberation of the serfs in 1867. Further developed at the end of the 19th century, it is currently one of the largest prisons in Europe with 960 cells—and a history of appalling overcrowding, its population reaching 12,500 in the mid-1990s. Readers of Solzhenitsyn's *The First Circle* will be familiar with the principle of the *sharashka,* secret research laboratories within GULAG camps: there was one here, the OKB-172 facility, developing torpedo boats later used in WWII. The 1884–1890 red brick building is appropriately Gothic, but this is a site more appropriately viewed from a distance. It's open to the public, with a museum detailing its most famous former residents, and offers tours of current inmates' quarters. But you won't get any help from me. *Arsenalnaya Nab. d. 5–7. Metro: Ploshad Lenina.* ●

3 The Best Neighborhood Walks

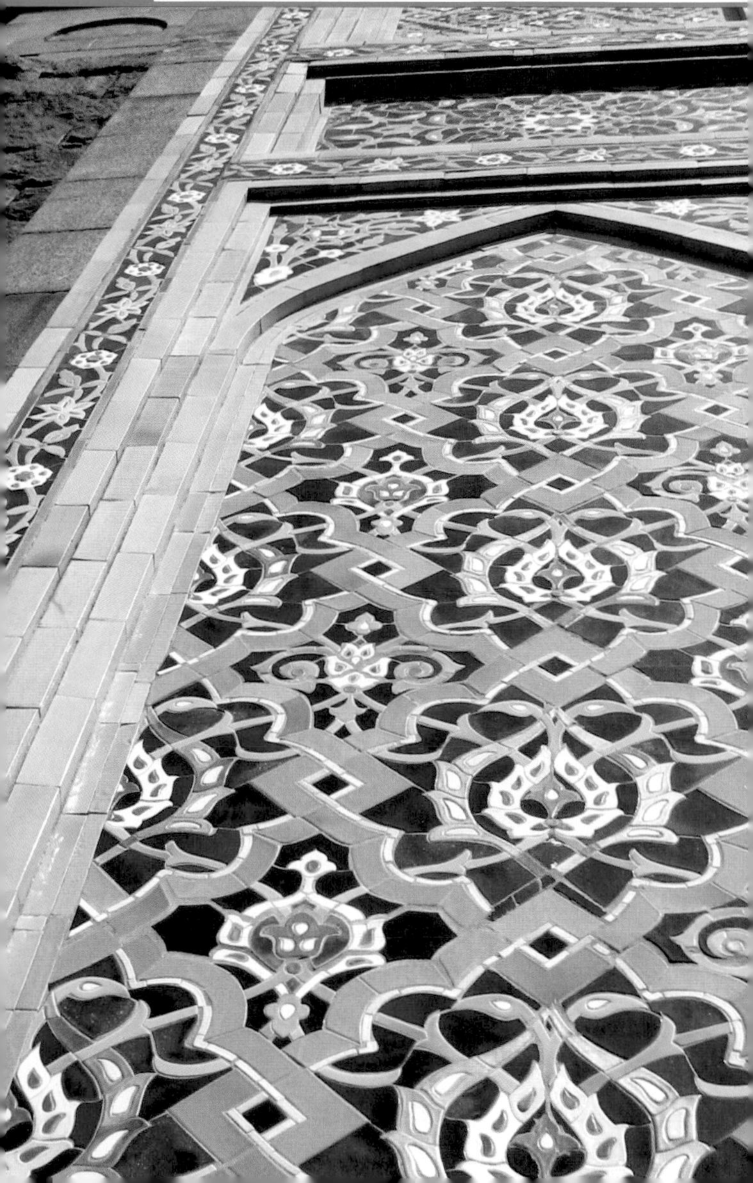

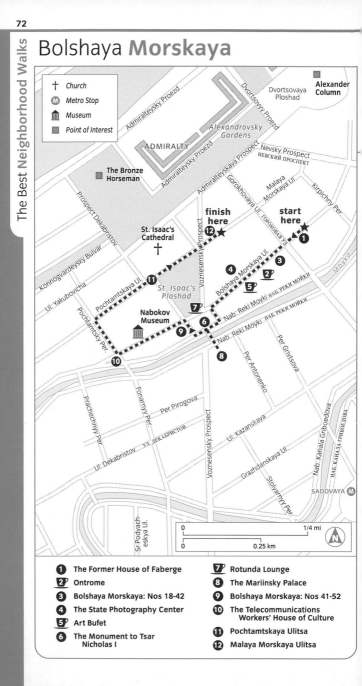

Bolshaya **Morskaya**

1 The Former House of Faberge

2 Ontrome

3 Bolshaya Morskaya: Nos 18-42

4 The State Photography Center

5 Art Bufet

6 The Monument to Tsar
   Nicholas I

7 Rotunda Lounge

8 The Mariinsky Palace

9 Bolshaya Morskaya: Nos 41-52

10 The Telecommunications
   Workers' House of Culture

11 Pochtamtskaya Ulitsa

12 Malaya Morskaya Ulitsa

This tour, along one of the city's most famous streets, historically populated by aristocrats, musicians, and artists, takes in some stunning Style Moderne and Art Deco friezes, historic sites (including those of Dostoevsky's arrest and Tchaikovsky's death), a few quirky museums and a multitude of snack spots. START: **From Nevsky Prospect metro. But take the scenic route, via Bolshaya Konnushennaya and a beer at the James Cook pub, cutting through Volinsky Pereulok to the other side of the Moika.**

❶ The Former House of Faberge (Yakhont Jewelers). Jewelers to the Imperial Court from 1885, when the first Fabergé egg was commissioned by Tsar Alexander II for his wife, Maria Fyodorovna, the Fabergé company was founded in 1842 and originally located on the other side of the street at No. 11. Fifty-seven eggs were produced in total, of which 21 remain in Russia (11 of them in the Kremlin Armory), nine of them purchased by Russian oil magnate Victor Vekselberg in 2004. The actual jewels on sale here now aren't that impressive: but the building is, with a pristine Style Moderne interior and a Museum of Jewelry (appointment only). *B. Morskaya Ul. d. 24.* ☎ *812 314 6415. AE, DC, MC, V. Metro: Nevsky Prospect. Map p 72.*

The State Photography Center.

❷ Ontrome. The first of many coffee-and-cake refuelling stops along this stretch. French patisserie and good coffee, reasonably priced. *B. Morskaya Ul. d. 36.* ☎ *812 315 5030. $.*

❸ ★★ Bolshaya Morskaya: Nos 18–42. You might not think so from the austere Technical Design Institute facing you as you leave Nevsky, but this stretch has some of the most picturesque buildings in town. Don't miss the Union of Russian Artists at No. 38 (originally built in the 1890s for the Art Encouragement Fund) and the Russian Insurance Society buildings at No. 35 and No. 37.

❹ ★★★ The State Photography Center. Personally I wouldn't

bother with the exhibitions: but the mosaics on this Style Moderne mansion are more than matched by the architecture inside. Take the lift to the top floor to make your way down past Art Nouveau stained glass windows on every landing, and the eerie plaster bas reliefs on the ground floor: don't miss the walrus above your head on your way out. *Rosfoto, B. Morskaya Ul. d. 35. ☎ 812 314 1214. Admission 100R.*

5 **Art Bufet.** Style Moderne and stained glass in the building of the former Art Encouragement Society. *B. Morskaya Ul. d. 38. ☎ 812 944 2204. $.*

6 **The Monument to Tsar Nicholas I.** Auguste de Montferrand's 1856 statue of one of the most reactionary and unpopular Tsars (born 1796, and ruling from 1825–1855) was erected by his successor, Alexander II. Popular subscription was never likely to be on the cards, Nicholas I having been responsible for the suppression of the Decembrist revolt (see p 172),

and the establishment of the Third Department (political police) and the creation of the brutal Corps of Gendarmes.

7 **Rotunda Lounge.** Astoria Hotel. At 1,050 rubles, the afternoon tea here isn't cheap. But it is the height of indulgence, with a chocolate fountain and blini cooked to order. *B. Morskaya Ul. d 39. ☎ 812 494 5137. $$$$.*

8 **The Mariinsky Palace.** Now home to the St Petersburg Legislative Assembly, this Neoclassical building was originally built (1839–1844) for Grand Princess Maria Nikolaevna, daughter of Nicholas I. Legend has it that she was outraged when her father's statue was erected with the horse's rear end directly facing the palace. The grim Constructivist building to the right of it is the Office of the Procurator General: take no photos. Plaques on Isaakievskaya Ploshad d. 9 nearby show that this was once home to French Enlightenment philosopher Denis Diderot and avant garde

Tsar Nicholas I.

painter Kazimir Malevich, whose *Black Square* can be found in the Hermitage (see p 26).

9 ★★ Bolshaya Morskaya: Nos 41–52. Another stretch of elegant façades, including the Baroque Dom Demidova at No. 43 (architect Montferrand 1835–1840), and the Dom Kompositorov next door at No. 45. Directly opposite the Nabokov Museum at No. 49 (see p 46) stands the Polovtsov House (No. 52). Now the Dom Arkitektorov, the original building dates from the early 18th century, its façades remodeled in 1888.

10 ★★★ The Telecommunications Workers' House of Culture. Built in 1932–1939 (architects P.M. Grinberg and G.S. Rayts) where the German Reformed Church had once stood, it's worth walking right round this building to appreciate the very Soviet bas reliefs on what was once a typical *Dom Kultury* (House of Culture). Keep going south past the Potseluyev (Kissing) Bridge and turn right into Konnogvardeisky Pereulok where you'll find another piece of derelict Constructivism directly on the corner with Pochtamtskaya Ulitsa. *B. Morskaya Ul. d. 58.*

11 Pochtamtskaya Ulitsa. So called for the central post office at No. 9, there are two museums on this street, which might be of interest to some: the A.S. Popov Central Museum of Communications and the Museum of the History of Religion. Personally I find both hard going, although the latter occasionally has good temporary exhibitions, notably one covering the Freemasons, in 2008. *The A.S. Popov Central Museum of Communications, Pochtamtskaya Ul. d. 7.* ☎ *812 571 0060. www.*

Telecommunications Workers' House of Culture.

rustelecom-museum.ru. Admission 70R adults, 30R kids. 10.30am–6pm, closed Sun–Mon. The Museum of the History of Religion, Pochtamtskaya Ul. d. 14. ☎ *812 312 3586. Admission 120R adults, 30R kids. 11am–6pm, closed Wed. Metro: Gostiny Dvor, then buses 3, 22, 27.*

12 Malaya Morskaya Ulitsa. This final stretch is a goldmine for culture buffs. No. 25 was the scene of Dostoevsky's arrest in 1849 (see p 46); Nikolai Gogol wrote *Diary of a Madman* and *The Nose* at No. 17, and Pyotr Tchaikovsky died at No. 13: most likely from cholera and not, as some claim, by suicide over discovery of his homosexuality. Almost directly opposite this building (at No. 10) is the 'Queen of Spades' house, once the residence of Princess Golitsyna, said to be the inspiration for Pushkin's novella (and later Tchaikovsky's opera) of the same name.

Nevsky Prospect

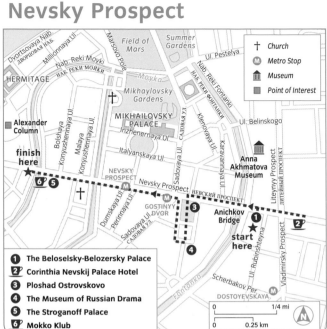

Legend:
- † Church
- Ⓜ Metro Stop
- 🏛 Museum
- ▪ Point of Interest

① The Beloselsky-Belozersky Palace
② Corinthia Nevskij Palace Hotel
③ Ploshad Ostrovskovo
④ The Museum of Russian Drama
⑤ The Stroganoff Palace
☕ Mokko Klub

0 — 1/4 mi
0 — 0.25 km

Victim of this decade's retail and property boom in the city, the scaffolding lining Nevsky Prospect hasn't left it looking its best. Uncover some hidden gems on the main stretch, then lose yourself in the Gothic turn-of-the-century buildings at its northern end. START: **From Mayakovskaya metro towards the Anichkov Bridge.**

① The Beloselsky–Belozersky Palace. Now the property of the Presidential Administration, tours of this Neo-Baroque palace built in 1848 are only possible on odd (and erratic) dates: you'll find them posted in the ticket office in the basement. Stick your head round the door, however, for a stunning interior of gilt, mirrors, and innumerable plasterwork Atlantes. Hard to believe this was, until 1991, the location of the *RaiKom* (district council). *Nevsky Prospect d. 41.* ☎ *812 315 5236.*

② Corinthia Nevskij Palace Hotel. The coffee chains that dominate Nevsky are shockingly bad value in European and American eyes. This hotel might look expensive, but you'll get more than your money's worth at the Bierstube restaurant's 880-ruble 'business lunch' buffet. *Nevsky Prospect d. 57.* ☎ *812 334 1650. $.*

③ ★★ Ploshad Ostrovskovo. Don't limit yourself to the Catherine the Great statue and the veteran chess players in the gardens. Have

Nevsky Backstreets

Once notorious for the backstreets immortalized in *Crime and Punishment* (see p 45), the city, alas, gets ever more sanitized, with even Dostoevsky's old stomping ground now awash with neon. Find some of the most Gothic buildings and *dvors* (courtyards) in the Vladimirskaya district at Nevsky's northernmost end, dotted with 'alternative' shops, bars, and eccentric eateries. Head along Ul. Rubinsteina (stopping for drinks at the **Chainy Dom**, see p 125), then into Kolokolnaya Ul. for the Russian Revival apartment building at No. 11, and two others in Povarskoi Pereulok (Nos 8 and 14). Don't miss the gold-lettered building at Stremyana Ul. d. 20: the former bookstore of the **Society for Religious and Moral Education**.

your portrait painted at the open-air art market outside the catholic Church of St Catherine at No. 32–34, then trace the exotic façades that line the square: from the State Transport Service at No. 2, round to the masks on the Alexandrinsky Theater administration building.

4 kids **The Museum of Russian Drama.** Tucked away at the rear of the Alexandrinsky Theater, the costume displays here might prove a welcome diversion for junior drama queens. *Alexandrinsky Theater, Ploshad Ostrovskovo. ☎ 812 710 4176. www.alexandrinsky.ru.*

5 ★★ **The Stroganoff Palace.** Ignore the waxworks museum and the hilariously over-designed café in the courtyard: the entrance to the main palace is further down on your left, the city's only Rastrelli building still fully intact. *Nevsky Prospect d. 17. ☎ 812 571 8238. www.rusmuseum.ru.*

6 **Mokko Klub.** A warm and cozy 24-hour bar: the perfect refuge from a Nevsky rainstorm. *Nevsky Prospect d. 17. ☎ 812 312 1080. $.*

The Beloselsky-Belozersky Palace.

Vasilievsky **Island**

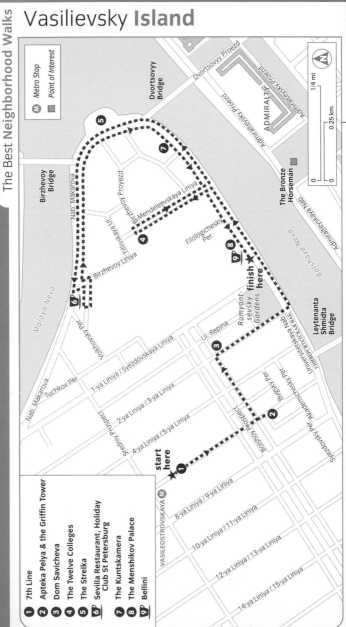

Legend:
- ⓜ Metro Stop
- ■ Point of Interest

1 7th Line
2 Apteka Pelya & the Griffin Tower
3 Dom Savicheva
4 The Twelve Colleges
5 The Strelka
6 Sevilla Restaurant, Holiday Club St Petersburg
7 The Kuntskamera
8 The Menshikov Palace
9 Bellini

Domenico Trezzini's 1716 plan to build Peter I's new city on a geometric Venetian canal grid never came to fruition, alas. But his intentions are quite clear in this district's meticulously numbered *liniya* (lines). With its early Petrine architecture and panoramic views across the Neva, this must be the most picturesque quarter of the city. Go in the early morning or on a late White Night, and watch the sky turn to dusky shades of pink, violet, and gold. START: **From Vasileostrovsky metro.**

1 ★ **7th Line.** Miss this if you're in a hurry (take bus 1 or 7 from Nevsky Prospect direct to the Strelka), but this cafe-lined pedestrian street is one of the city's best strolling spots, from the horse-drawn tram to the St Andrew Cathedral, the last Baroque church to be built in the city. The obelisk in front commemorates the tercentenary of the Order of St Andrew, in whose honor the church was established by Peter I.

2 ★ **Apteka Pelya & the Griffin Tower.** Architecturally, this turn-of-the-century former pharmacy is of interest as a classic piece of Style Moderne (built in 1907–1910). The urban myths surrounding it, however, are mind-boggling. Try and get into the courtyard, where you'll find a red-brick tower,

covered with scribbled numbers. The encrypted code to the universe, according to some, or the result of a perestroika artistic installation, according to others. Another myth has it that invisible griffins fly into the tower at night, seen only through images reflected in the windows of neighboring houses. The pharmacy was established in 1858 and supplied the Imperial Court. Another myth suggests Alexander Pel in fact achieved notoriety through his invention of an early version of Viagra, made from pig semen. *7th Line, d. 16.*

3 **Dom Savicheva.** Revered in Russia as deeply as Anne Frank, Tanya Savicheva's Siege diary records—with the bewildered directness of an 11-year-old

The Twelve Colleges.

child—the deaths of all members of her family. Her last entry reads: 'The Savichevs have all died. Only Tanya is left'. She herself died, after evacuation, in 1944. Copies of her diary entries can be seen in the Rumyantsev Mansion (see p 49). *2nd Line, d. 13.*

④ ★★ The Twelve Colleges.

Although they now form part of St Petersburg State University, this 440-meter complex (originally comprising 12 individual buildings, built by Domenico Trezzini, 1721–1744) housed the 12 ministries of Peter the Great's government. Follow its full length along the Mendeleevk-saya Liniya to find a statue of the Nobel Prize-winning physicist and dissident in Sakharov Square. *Universitetskaya Nab. d. 7.*

⑤ ★★★ The Strelka. Your eye

will immediately be drawn to Thomas de Thomon's Rostral Columns (built in 1805–1810) in front of the former Stock Exchange that dominates Birzhevaya (Exchange) Square. The ships' prows on each of the columns represent Russia's main rivers—the Volga, the Dnieper, the Neva, and the Volkhov. Be sure

The Kunstkamera.

to walk the full length of the Strelka (*Spit*): you'll find a very helpful relief map showing all of the buildings facing the Neva.

⑥ Sevilla Restaurant, Holiday Club St Petersburg. A new open-

ing in late 2008, the Monday-to-Friday lunch buffet is a bargain at 595 rubles. *Birzhevoi Per. d. 2–4, V.O.* ☎ *812 335 2200. $$.*

⑦ ★★★ The Kunstkamera. The

main attraction for most will be the 'Cabinet of Naturalia', Peter I's brave attempt to educate the nation through the (enforced) collection of still-born and malformed children and animals in the country's first museum. There's more to the Kunstkamera than this ghoul-fest, however. The tower was used in the 18th century as the country's first astronomical observatory, and much of that early equipment is displayed on the fourth floor, including the early telescope through which Lomonosov was able to track the passage of Venus across the sun. Don't miss the Great Gottorp Globe on the floor above: 3.1 meters in diameter, and illustrated inside with one of the world's earliest maps of the cosmos. The globe was constructed in 1654–1664 and given to Peter the Great during the Great Northern War; it was retrieved (or more accurately, seized) by the Germans in 1941, before being returned in 1947. *Universitetskaya Nab. d. 3.* ☎ *812 328 1412. www. kunstkamera.ru. Admission 200R adults, 100R kids. 11am–6pm, closed Mon and last Tues. Metro: Vasileo-strovskaya, or Nevsky Prospect then bus 7 or 10, trolleybus 1,7,10.*

⑧ ★ The Menshikov Palace.

Built for the first Governor of St. Petersburg (and Peter I's long-standing companion), Alexander

The Menshikov Palace.

Menshikov, this building was constructed in 1710–1721, although development continued until Menshikov's exile to Siberia in 1727. Visit as part of your inclusive two-day Hermitage ticket: the must-sees are the tiled Marine Study and the Walnut Room. *Universitetskaya Nab. d. 15.* ☎ *812 323 1112. 10.30 am-6pm daily (to 5pm Sun, closed Mon).*

9 Bellini. A new opening in December 2008, ignore the restaurant for perfect, 100-rubles-a-cup Italian coffee in its very stylish lobby bar. *Universitetskaya Nab. d. 13.* ☎ *812 331 1001. $.*

The Maritime City

It's some distance west, but this stretch of the Lieutenant Schmidt embankment can provide a good day's entertainment for kids. Summer sees the Yunniy Baltiets tall ship and an S-189 submarine (shortly to be refitted as a museum) moored along the Neva. It's due to relocate to the former naval barracks in New Holland, but you might just catch the **Central Naval Museum** in its current illustrious premises in the former Stock Exchange Building (Birzhevaya Ploshad d. 4, ☎ 328 2501). Junior mariners will enjoy exploring the British-built **Icebreaker Krasin**, once the largest breaker in the world, Nab. Lieutenanta Schmidta, 21-aya Liniya VSO. ☎ 812 325 3546, ☎ 812 325 3547. www.krassin.ru/en/ice_breaker), or better still, the **'People's Will' D-2 Submarine** (Shkipersky Protok d. 10. ☎ 812 356 5277, ☎ 812 356 5266).

Workers' **Paradise**

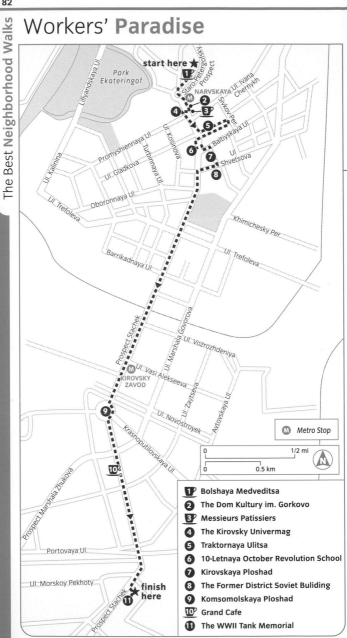

start here ★

Park Ekaterinof

NARVSKAYA

1 Bolshaya Medveditsa

2 The Dom Kultury im. Gorkovo

3 Messieurs Patissiers

4 The Kirovsky Univermag

5 Traktornaya Ulitsa

6 10-Letnaya October Revolution School

7 Kirovskaya Ploshad

8 The Former District Soviet Buliding

9 Komsomolskaya Ploshad

10 Grand Cafe

11 The WWII Tank Memorial

M Metro Stop

finish here ★

0   1/2 mi
0   0.5 km

N

Emerging from Narvskaya metro onto Prospect Stachek is to step back into the glory days of Soviet central planning: the classic Constructivist Gorky Palace of Culture, the 10-Letnaya Oktyabr School (built in the shape of a hammer and sickle), the experimental workers' housing of Tractornaya Ulitsa, and the pristine layout of Kirovskaya Ploshad all evocative of a time when many hoped the century's bravest experiment might actually work. Architecture fans and historians will be in their element: everyone else will enjoy a two-hour stroll through one of the city's eeriest corners.

START: **Narvskaya metro, bearing directly left for the Dom Kultury im. Gorkovo.**

1 **kids** **Bolshaya Medveditsa.** It's politically incorrect of course, but kids will love the real (stuffed) polar bear in this bistro. *Staro-Peterhofsky Prospect d. 43/45/* ☎ *812 786 6139,* ☎ *812 746 6780. $.*

2 ★★★ **The Dom Kultury im. Gorkovo.** Possibly due to the importance of the Kirovsky Zavod in the city's revolutionary history (see below), the *Kirovsky rayon* (district) became, after the Revolution, one of the most important social and community centers of the city. At some pains to minimize the stark contrast between the aristocratic center and this very working-class neighborhood, it was almost immediately redeveloped according to the principles of the day. A new layout for the area was drafted as early as 1924, based around ploshads Stachek (Square of Strikes) and Kirovskaya (named for Sergei Kirov, an early Bolshevik and participant in the 1905 revolt, whose assassination in 1934 was to trigger the Great Terror). This 'Palace of Culture'—the first in the Soviet Union—was completed for the 10th anniversary of the Revolution, 1927: it is still a working venue, albeit with a high preponderance of Russian-language musicals and comedies. Directly next to this is another classic Constructivist building, the former

Institute of Professional-Technical Education (now in some disrepair and home to a very Soviet furniture store), at Ul. Ivan Chernykh No. 4. Don't miss the propagandist mural ('Workers of the World Unite!') on the wall of Ul. Ivan Chernykh No. 2. *Prospect Stachek d. 4.* ☎ *812 252 7513. Metro: Narvskaya.*

3 **Messieurs Patissiers.** Good coffee, authentic French pastries, and a wide range of cheap hot snacks. *Prospect Stachek d. 2/2.* ☎ *812 786 7322,* ☎ *8 901 302 8798. $.*

Sergei Kirov: popular party chief and the first victim of Stalin's Great Terror.

4 ★★ The Kirovsky Univermag. It's somewhat compromised nowadays by the McDonald's and other logos that festoon its façades, but this Constructivist monolith, built in 1929–1931, is still identifiable as the department store and communal canteen it once was, producing up to 15,000 meals a day for distribution to the city's factories, even during the Siege. *Kirovsky Univermag, Prospect Stachek d. 9.*

5 ★★★ Traktornaya Ulitsa. This tiny estate of three-storey houses was the epitome of the Constructivist garden city, built in 1925–1927 by architects A.I. Gegello, A.S. Nikolsky, and G.A. Simonov. The elegant arches, with every apartment block divided by a strip of garden, give a hint of the workers' paradise originally intended for this model district. Gegello, incidentally, was the architect responsible for the Dom Kultury im. Gorkovo: yet another of his buildings, the Dvorets Kultury i Tekhniki im. Ivan Gaza (named for the early Bolshevik agitator whose statue stands directly in front), is at Prospect Stachek No. 72.

6 ★★★ 10-Letnaya October Revolution School. The first school to be built in the city after the Revolution, again completed for its 10th anniversary in 1927, it was perhaps inevitable that this would be a propagandist affair. Architects A.S. Nikolsky and A.V. Krestin surpassed themselves, however, by building the entire complex in the shape of a hammer and sickle. Still a functioning school (nowadays known simply as School No. 384), it's best viewed from behind. Keep going right and nip through the railings—no one will stop you. *Prospect Stachek d. 5.*

7 Kirovskaya Ploshad. Leading Constructivist architect Ivan A. Fomin developed the plans for this square in 1919. The statue in front,

The former District Soviet building.

The WWII Tank Memorial.

of Leningrad party head Sergei Kirov, was erected in 1938: somewhat ironically, at the height of the Stalinist purges unleashed by his assassination four years earlier.

❽ The Former District Soviet Building. Unmissable, its neon-lit hammer and sickle untouched by perestroika or Putinism, this massive Constructivist complex was built in 1930–1935 by architect N.A. Trotsky. Its 2,000-capacity convention hall was converted in 1958 to include the 'Progress' cinema: currently under reconstruction, it is rumored it will reopen as a business center.

❾ Komsomolskaya Ploshad. It's quite a trek from top to bottom, but Prospect Stachek's parks hold some classic pieces of Soviet statuary. Ekateringhof Park (once a country estate of Peter I's wife Catherine, renamed in 1948 as the Thirtieth Anniversary of the All-Union Leninist Communist Youth League Park) has a very ornate statue commemorating the Krasnodon Young Guard, an underground Komsomol organization in the Ukraine, many members of which were executed by the Germans in 1943. Further south, just beyond Komsomolskaya Ploshad, you will find another, commemorating the fiftieth anniversary of the All-Union Leninist Communist Youth League (or Komsomol), erected in 1968.

❿ Grand Cafe. It looks imposing, but this is actually a cozy independent café, with original art for sale on the walls. *Prospect Stachek d. 67.* ☎ *812 784 5094. $.*

⓫ The WWII Tank Memorial. The Siege frontline ran very close to the Narvskaya district. See p 48 for the full tour, or catch the No. K66, K45, K424 marshrutka to Prospect Stachek d. 108, where you'll find the Victory Tank Memorial (as well as a former bunker) and a wartime tram-car.

Petrogradskaya

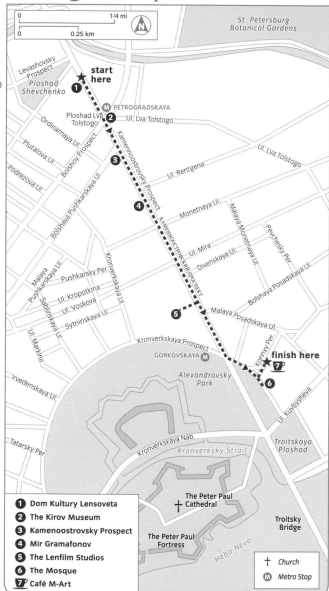

start here

St. Petersburg
Botanical Gardens

Levashovsky
Prospect

Ploshad
Shevchenko

1

Ⓜ PETROGRADSKAYA

Ploshad Lva
Tolstogo **2**

Ul. Lva Tolstogo

Ordinarnaya Ul.

Ul. Lva Tolstogo

Plutalova Ul.

3

Kamennoostrovsky Prospect

Podrezova Ul.

Bolshoy Prospect

Ul. Rentgena

4

Monetnaya Ul.

Bolshaya Pushkarskaya Ul.

Malaya Pushkarskaya Ul.

Kronverkskaya Ul.

Ul. Mira

Malaya Monetnaya Ul.

Pevchesky Per.

Pushkarsky Per.

Divenskaya Ul.

Ul. Kropotkina

Sablinskaya Ul.

Ul. Voskova

Bolshaya Posadskaya Ul.

Sytninskaya Ul.

5

Malaya Posadskaya Ul.

Ul. Markina

Kronverkskaya Prospect

GORKOVSKAYA Ⓜ

Konnvy Per.

finish here

7

6

Vvedenskaya Ul.

Alexandrovsky
Park

Ul. Kuybysheva

Tatarsky Per.

Kronverkskaya Nab.

Kronverksky Strait

Troitskaya
Ploshad

The Peter Paul
✝ Cathedral

Troitsky
Bridge

The Peter Paul
Fortress

Heba Neva

1 Dom Kultury Lensoveta
2 The Kirov Museum
3 Kamenoostrovsky Prospect
4 Mir Gramafonov
5 The Lenfilm Studios
6 The Mosque
7 Café M-Art

✝ Church
Ⓜ Metro Stop

0   1/4 mi
0   0.25 km

The opening of the Troitsky Bridge in 1903 gave rise to the many Style Moderne buildings that dominate this district: luxurious apartment houses *(dohodniye doma)* built for the beneficiaries of the city's rapid industrialization. The 'Golden Triangle' might be the most glamorous district, and Vasilievsky Island the most picturesque, but this quarter, dotted with eccentric museums, is my favorite place for simply getting lost. START: **On scenic main street Kamenoostrovsky Prospect, direct from the Petrogradskaya metro.**

❶ Dom Kultury Lensoveta. Built in 1930–1938, this striking late Constructivist monolith will hit you as soon as you emerge from the metro. *Kamenoostrovsky Prospect d. 42.* ☎ *812 346 0438,* ☎ *812 346 3063. Ticket prices vary. Metro: Petrogradskaya. Map p 86.*

❷ ★★ The Kirov Museum. The apartment of the one-time Leningrad party chief and protégé of Stalin (at least until he engineered his assassination in 1934), at a time when almost all Stalinist memorabilia has been scrupulously removed from public view, the sheer number of Stalin portraits in this museum comes as something of a shock. Worse still are the staggering inequities it highlights of the early Soviet period: originally owned by the First Russian Insurance Society, while the rest of the post-Revolution population was crammed into *communalki* (shared apartments), this house (built in 1914 with all the conveniences of running water, sanitation, and electricity) was reserved for members of the party elite. The *Take What You're Given* exhibition (covering the food distribution system of the late 1920s) also highlights the appalling disparities between *rabochiye* (workers') and

spetz (party members') rations. Take the stairs on your way down: on the second floor you'll find a notice advertising the Petrograd district office of the Federal Security Service—or, as we used to call it, the KGB. *Kamenoostrovsky Prospect d. 26–28.* ☎ *812 346-02-17,* ☎ *346-02-89. http://kirovmuseum.spb.ru/eng Admission 70R adults, 40R kids. 11am–6pm (to 5pm Tues), closed Wed. Metro: Petrogradskaya then bus 46.*

❸ ★ Kamenoostrovsky Prospect. The most famous of this district's Style Moderne buildings, Constantine Rozenstein and Andrei Belogrud's 1913 'Turreted House' (at Ul. Lev Tolstova d. 2) was under scaffolding as we went to print. Keep going south, however, for newly restored façades on Avstriskaya Ploshad.

❹ Mir Gramafonov. I can give you no idea of what goes on in this museum, the attendant having been 'too busy' to let me in. Enquiring about ticket prices, I was told: 'Two hundred and fifty rubles—but for foreigners, even more!' Perhaps one for antiques fans only, or anyone wanting to sample

The Lenfilm Studios.

Spectacular mosaics on the Mosque.

the undying tradition of Soviet customer service. *B. Pushkarskaya Ul. d. 47.* ☎ *812 346 0951,* ☎ *8 905 219 5699.*

⑤ The Lenfilm Studios. There's little to see, and the overzealous *dezhurnaya* (attendant) will chase you if you try to get any further than the lobby. Nonetheless, film buffs might want to pay homage to the home of Soviet cinematographic classics including *Chapayev* and *20 Days Without War*. Located on the site of Russia's first public film screening in 1896, the original cinema (in the courtyard to the right of the main building) is now, inevitably, a DVD and video shop. *Kamenoostrovsky Prospect d. 10.* ☎ *812 326-83-41* ☎ *232-88-81. www.lenfilm.ru.*

⑥ ★★★ The Mosque. The Tatars of Nizhny Novgorod and Kazan had been instrumental in building the early city of Peter the Great, and a thriving market and Tatar *sloboda* (settlement) quickly grew up around the Kronverk, where the mosque now stands. Built to commemorate the 25th anniversary of the reign of the last Emir of Bukhara, and inspired by the tomb of Tamerlane in Samarkand, it opened in 1921, was used as a warehouse during WWII, and returned to the Muslim community in 1956. A decade of restoration has resulted in a pristine interior: the mosaics above the main entrance, in particular, are stunning. You might want to retrace your steps to see the former mansion of the Emir of Bukhara, incidentally, at Kamenoostrovsky Prospect d. 44. *Kronverksky Prospect d. 7.* ☎ *812 233 9819.*

⑦ Café M-Art. A minimalist haven, next door to the mosque, with a cup of coffee for less than 100 rubles. *Konniy Per. d. 1.* ☎ *812 233 1013.* ●

Shopping Best Bets

Best for **Amber**
★★ Northway, *Angliiskaya Naberezhnaya d. 36 (p 98)*

Best for **Antiques**
★★★ Antikvariat, *M. Morskaya d. 21 (p 94)*

Best for **Art**
Dom Knigi, *Nevsky Prospect d. 28 (p 95)*

Best for **Bling**
Khlebnikov Jewelry Salon, *Nevsky Prospect d. 29/31 (p 97)*

Best for **Books in English**
★★ Knizhaya Lavka, *Nevsky Prospect d. 66 (p 95)*

Best for **Booze**
Legendi Ararat, *Vladimirsky Prospect d. 13/9 (p 100)*

Best for **Busts (Lenin's)**
Chocolate Museum, *Nevsky Prospect d. 62 (p 95)*

Best for **Caviar**
Lend Supermarket, *Vladimirsky Passazh, Vladimirsky Prospect d. 19 (p 100)*

Best for **Flowers**
★★★ Dom Tsvetov, *Bolshaya Konushennaya Ulitsa d. 12 (p 96)*

Best for **Lomonosov China**
★★★ Imperial Porcelain, *Vladimirsky Prospect d. 7 (p 95)*

Best for **Pre-Revolutionary Glamor**
★★★ Dom Knigi, *Nevsky Prospect d. 28 (p 95)*

Best for **Propaganda (Posters)**
Bukvoed, *Ligovsky Prospect d. 10 (p 95)*

Best **Shop-'til-you-drop Sugar Boost**
Sever, *Nevsky Prospect d. 44 (p 96)*

Best for **Souvenirs**
★★★ Vernisazh, *Naberezhnaya Kanala Griboedova d. 1 (p 100)*

Best for **Soviet Kitsch**
★★★ Pioneer Shop, *Periniye Liniya Shopping Center, Dumskaya Ulitsa d. 4. (p 97)*

The busy Nevsky Prospect.

The Northern Islands **Shopping**

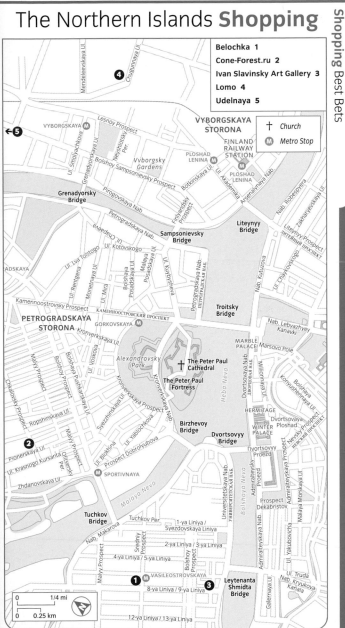

Belochka **1**
Cone-Forest.ru **2**
Ivan Slavinsky Art Gallery **3**
Lomo **4**
Udelnaya **5**

† Church
Ⓜ Metro Stop

VYBORGSKAYA STORONA

FINLAND RAILWAY STATION

PLOSHAD LENINA

Vyborgsky Gardens

Grenadyorsky Bridge

Sampsonievsky Bridge

Liteynyy Bridge

PETROGRADSKAYA STORONA

GORKOVSKAYA Ⓜ

Alexandrovsky Park

The Peter Paul Cathedral

The Peter Paul Fortress

Troitsky Bridge

MARBLE PALACE   Marsovo Pole

HERMITAGE

WINTER PALACE

Birzhevoy Bridge

Dvortsovyy Bridge

SPORTIVNAYA Ⓜ

Malaya Neva

Tuchkov Bridge

Bolshaya Neva

Prospect Dekabristov

VASILEOSTROVSKAYA Ⓜ

Leytenanta Shmidta Bridge

0   1/4 mi
0   0.25 km

Shopping West of Nevsky

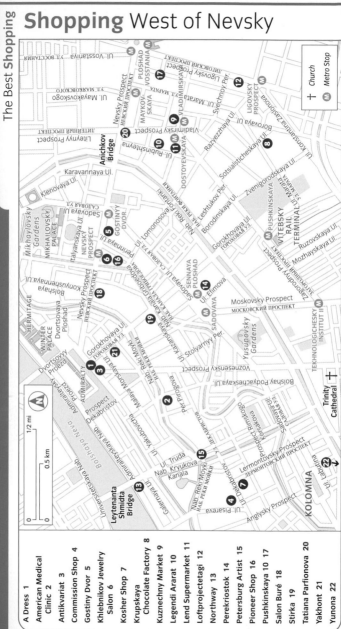

Church
Metro Stop

A Dress 1
American Medical
Clinic 2
Antikvariat 3
Commission Shop 4
Gostiny Dvor 5
Khlebnikov Jewelry
Salon 6
Kosher Shop 7
Krupskaya
Chocolate Factory 8
Kuznechny Market 9
Legendi Ararat 10
Lend Supermarket 11
Loftprojectetagi 12
Northway 13
Perekriostok 14
Petersburg Artist 15
Pioneer Shop 16
Pushkinskaya 10 17
Salon Buré 18
Stirka 19
Tatiana Parfionova 20
Yakhont 21
Yunona 22

Shopping East of Nevsky

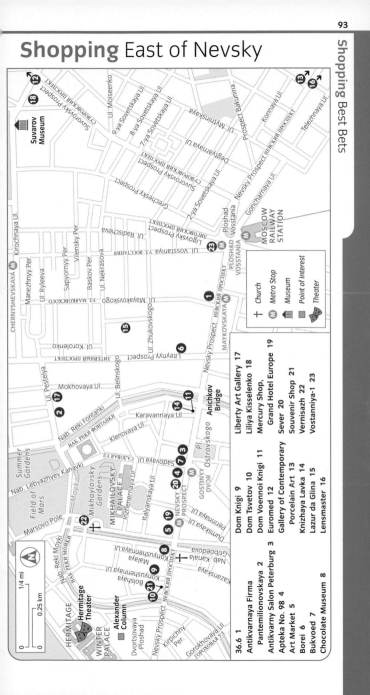

Suvarov Museum

CHERNYSHEVSKAYA

PLOSHAD VOSSTANIA

MOSCOW RAILWAY STATION

MAYKOVSKAYA

GOSTINNY DVOR

NEVSKY PROSPECT

Anichkov Bridge

Summer Gardens

Field of Mars

Marsovo Pole

MIKHAYLOVSKY PALACE

Mikhaylovsky Gardens

Hermitage Theater

WINTER PALACE

Alexander Column

Dvortsovaya Ploshad

Legend:
+ Church
Ⓜ Metro Stop
🏛 Museum
■ Point of Interest
🎭 Theater

36.6 1
Antikvarnaya Firma
Pantemilionovskaya 2
Antikvarny Salon Peterburg 3
Apteka No. 98 4
Art Market 5
Borei 6
Bukvoed 7
Chocolate Museum 8

Dom Knigi 9
Dom Tsvetov 10
Dom Voennoi Knigi 11
Euromed 12
Gallery of Contemporary
  Porcelain Art 13
Knizhaya Lavka 14
Lazur da Glina 15
Lensmaster 16

Liberty Art Gallery 17
Liliya Kisselenko 18
Mercury Shop,
  Grand Hotel Europe 19
Sever 20
Souvenir Shop 21
Vernisazh 22
Vostanniya-1 23

0 1/4 mi
0 0.25 km

St Petersburg **Shopping A to Z**

Antique Salons

Antikvariat ISAAKSIEVSKAYA PLOSHAD Looking (and smelling) exactly as an antique shop should, this is perfect for rummaging. This is the only place in Russia where I have ever found busts of Stalin's right-hand torturer Lavrenty Beria on sale. No reflection on themselves, they assure me, they simply take in goods to sell on commission. *M. Morskaya Ul. d. 21.* ☎ *812 571 2643. MC, V. Metro: Gostiny Dvor., Nevsky Prospect. Map p 92.*

Antikvarnaya Firma Pantemilionovskaya LITEINY PROSPECT An Alladin's cave of furniture, bronzes, and art. *Ul. Pestelya d. 13/15.* ☎ *812 579 6311. AE, DC, MC, V. Metro: Nevsky Prospect. Map p 93.*

Antikvarny Salon Peterburg NEVSKY PROSPECT Leningrad's first private antiques gallery, opened in 1988, selling art, furniture, icons, china, and glass from the 18th to the 20th centuries. *Nevsky Prospect d. 54.* ☎ *812 571 4020. AE, DC, MC, V. Metro: Gostiny Dvor. Map p 93.*

Borei LITEINY PROSPECT Antiquarian books (which you won't be able to export, so look, but don't buy), sketches, and handmade postcards. Closed Mon. *Liteiny Prospect d. 58.* ☎ *812 273 3693. AE, DC, MC, V. Metro: Mayakovskaya. Map p 93.*

Art Galleries

Ivan Slavinsky Art Gallery VASILIEVSKY OSTROV The city's first private gallery-museum (opened in 2007 by returned émigré Ivan Slavinsky) hosts regular retrospectives and exhibitions in addition to his own work. *5th Line VSO d. 5/5.* ☎ *812 328 2222,* ☎ *812 945 6810. http://ivan-slavinsky.com. AE, DC,* *MC, V. Metro: Vasileostrovskaya. Map p 91.*

Liberty Art Gallery LITEINY PROSPECT Specializing in socialist realist art from the 1930s to 1980s, its 'Born in the USSR' project aims to uncover and publicize the leading (and lesser known) artists of the Soviet period. The Northern Venice Art Gallery in the same building covers 17th–20th-century Russian and European art and antiques. *Ul. Pestelya d. 17/25.* ☎ *812 579 4410,* ☎ *812 579 2214. www.libertyart gallery.ru, www.nvgallery.ru. AE, DC, MC, V. Metro: Nevsky Prospect, Chernishevskaya. Map p 93.*

Loftprojectetagi LIGOVSKY PROSPECT Opened in 2007, this four-floor complex offers boutiques, galleries, the city's only organic restaurant, and the LoftWineBar— worth visiting on Wednesdays for its cinema screenings. *Ligovsky Prospect d. 74.* ☎ *812 458 5005. www.loftprojectetagi.ru. Metro: Ligovsky Prospect, Ploshad Vosstaniya. Map p 92.*

Petersburg Artist PLOSHAD TRUDA Opened in 2005, this gallery is dedicated to Russian art of the 1950s–1990s. Closed Sun–Tues. *Nab. Reki Moiki d.100.* ☎ *812 337 1339,* ☎ *812 314 0609. AE, DC, MC, V. Metro: Nevsky Prospect then marshrutkas K22, K169, K180 or buses 3, 22, 27. Map p 92.*

Pushkinskaya 10 NEVSKY PROSPECT A genuinely multicultural center (home to Fish Fabrique nightclub, the Gallery of Experimental Sound (GEZ), and the John Lennon museum), its numerous galleries include PhotoImage, Art Liga, and the Museum of Nonconformist Art. Closed Mon–Tues. *Pushkinskaya Ul. d. 10. (entrance via Ligovsky*

Prospect d. 53). ☎ *812 764 5371.*
http://en.p-10.ru/. Metro: Ploshad
Vosstaniya. Map p 92.

Books in English
Bukvoed NEVSKY PROSPECT
City-wide book chain, with a hilarious collection of Putin and Medve-
dev calendars, plates, and portraits.
This branch has an extensive selection of books in English, and a
24-hour café. *Ligovsky Prospect d.*
10. ☎ *812 601 0601. MC, V. Metro:*
Ploshad Vosstaniya. Map p 93.

Dom Knigi NEVSKY PROSPECT
An essential stop for streetmaps
and guides, but don't miss the fabu-
lous coffee table art books and
Soviet posters, all housed in one of
the city's most famous Style Mod-
erne buildings (see p 8, ❶). *Nevsky*
Prospect d. 28. ☎ *812 488 2355.*
MC, V. Metro: Nevsky Prospect.
Map p 93.

Dom Voennoi Knigi NEVSKY
PROSPECT   While the upper floors
are dedicated to the scientific and
military tomes from which it takes
its name, you'll find a good selection
of novels, humor, and travel guides
on the ground floor. *Nevsky Pros-*
pect d. 20. ☎ *812 312 4936. MC, V.*
Metro: Nevsky Prospect. Map p 93.

Knizhaya Lavka NEVSKY PROS-
PECT   The best bet for books in
English (from classic Russian novels
to chick-lit), as well as an extensive
collection on art and design, and a
good selection of Russian-language
first editions and antiques. *Nevsky*
Prospect d 66. ☎ *812 314 4818,*
☎ *812 314 4759. MC, V. Metro:*
Gostiny Dvor. Map p 93.

China & Glass
Gallery of Contemporary
Porcelain Art LOMONOSOV-
SKAYA   Re-opened in 2003 as a
division of the Hermitage, this
museum (within the Lomonosov

Dom Knigi.

factory) holds pieces dating back to
its establishment in 1744, including
designs by Avant Garde artists Malevich and Kandinsky. If you don't
have time to make the journey
south of town, head for the biggest
of its outlets on Vladimirsky Prospect. *Prospect Obukhovskoi Oborony*
d. 119. ☎ *812 326 1743; Vladimirsky*
Prospect d. 7. ☎ *812 560 8544. www.*
ipm.ru. MC, V. Metro: Lomonosov-
skaya. Map p 93.

Chocolate & Cakes
Belochka VASILIEVSKY
OSTROV   An old school *konditer-*
skaya with attitude to match. Stock
up on Soviet favorite Krasny Oktyabr
chocolates and crack-your-dentures
biscuits, but expect to get shouted
at when you pay at the *kassa*.
Sredny Prospect VSO, d. 28. ☎ *812*
323 1763. Rubles only. Metro:
Vasilieostrovskaya. Map p 91.

Chocolate Museum CITY-
WIDE   One of several branches
along Nevsky. Pick up a chocolate
Lenin for the folks at home. *Nevsky*
Prospect d. 62. ☎ *812 314 1656. MC,*
V. Metro: Gostiny Dvor. Map p 93.

Krupskaya Chocolate Factory

CITYWIDE   You'll find branches throughout the city, but this is the main factory outlet, named for Lenin's wife Nadezhda. Be warned: Russian chocolate is completely different to the European variety, dark, brittle and very sweet. *Sotsialisticheskaya Ul. d. 21.* ☎ *812 315 3286. www. krupskaya.com. MC, V. Metro: Ligovsky Prospect. Map p 92.*

Sever NEVSKY PROSPECT   Opened in 1903, this very traditional cake shop has traded through the Revolution, the Siege, and almost a century of communism. This branch, refurbished in summer 2008, has one of the city's cheapest cafés (with pots of tea from 109 rubles), as well as hundreds of cakes, all of them almost laughably extravagant in decoration and color. Forget all thoughts of e-numbers and indulge at least once. Free WiFi. *Nevsky Prospect d. 44.* ☎ *812 571 2589. MC, V. Metro: Mayakovskaya. Map p 93.*

Emergencies

36.6 NEVSKY PROSPECT   Part-owned by British pharmacy chain Boots, this is probably the most reliable source for Western and prescription medicines. Although the queues and service might eliminate any will to live. *Nevsky Prospect d. 98 (24-hrs).* ☎ *812 275 8187. MC, V. Metro: Mayakovskaya. Map p 93.*

American Medical Clinic

See p 169. *Map p 92.*

Apteka No. 98 NEVSKY PROSPECT   The city's first homeopathic pharmacy, established in 1833. Now somewhat worse for wear (with a deliciously dilapidated old-Soviet interior), but still offering a dedicated homeopathic prescription service and doctors' surgery. *Nevsky Prospect d. 50.* ☎ *812 571 4498. MC, V. Metro: Gostiny Dvor. Map p 93.*

Cone-Forest.ru DELIVERIES CITYWIDE   You can't drink the water, and if you're here for more than a couple of days you'll soon get pretty sick of dragging two-liter bottles home from the supermarket. Cone-Forest will deliver anywhere in the city within 24 hours. *B. Raznochinnaya Ul. d. 14 bldg. 5.* ☎ *812 448 6868. Rubles only. Metro: Chkalovskaya. Map p 91.*

Euromed See p 169. *Map p 93.*

Lensmaster PLOSHAD ALEXANDRA NEVSKOVO   A one-hour service as good as their word. *Moskva Mall, Ploshad Alexandra Nevskovo d. 2.* ☎ *812 676 0001. www.lensmaster.ru., MC, V. Metro: Ploshad Alexandra Nevskovo. Map p 93.*

Stirka GOROKHOVAYA   A launderette with live gigs, DJ sets, free WiFi,and an art club. Only in Russia. *Kazanskaya Ul. d. 26..* ☎ *812 314 5371. MC, V. Metro: Sennaya Ploshad. Map p 92.*

Vostanniya-1 NEVSKY PROSPECT   It might seem odd to include a digital copy center here, but Russian bureaucracy being what it is Trans-Siberian travelers (or anyone losing a passport) will appreciate this one-stop photo, copy, fax, and Internet shop, open until 10pm daily. *Ul. Vosstaniya d. 1.* ☎ *812 812 579 5770. AE, DC, MC, V. Metro: Ploshad Vosstaniya. Map p 93.*

Flowers

Dom Tsvetov NEVSKY PROSPECT   Russians take flower giving very seriously, and this luxurious oasis must have every variety under the sun. Go past the imported roses to find traditional English garden flowers, tiny hand posies for 100R, delicate and exotic flower-arranging accessories, and triffid-sized pot plants. *B. Konushennaya Ul. d. 12.*

Typical souvenir market stall.

☎ 812 315 8670. MC, V. Metro: Nevsky Prospect. Map p 93.

Gifts & Souvenirs

Commission Shop ULITSA DEKA-BRISTOV   Pure Soviet kitsch. *Ul. Dekabristov d. 49.* ☎ *812 714 0698. MC, V. Metro: Sadovaya, then marshrutka K1 or K306 to Anglisky Prospect. Map p 92.*

Lazur da Glina LITEINY PROSPECT   Sumptuous glazes on hand-crafted ceramics. *Ul. Chekhova d. 8.* ☎ *812 273 1729,* ☎ *812 967 2789. AE, DC, MC, V. Metro: Chernishevskaya. Map p 93.*

Lomo VYBORGSKAYA   Lomography is a cult photographic style popular since the 1990s, derived from the wide-angle, high-exposure shots achieved with the Lomo Kompakt Automat camera. While the company is these days better known for its high-spec medical and military equipment, hardened fans shouldn't miss the chance to visit the on-site museum. Closed Sat–Sun. *Chugunnaya Ul. d. 20.* ☎ *812 292 5242. AE, DC, MC, V. Metro: Vyborgskaya. Map p 91.*

★★★ Pioneer Shop NEVSKY PROSPECT   A very different proposition from the usual Lenin busts and fur hats. Genuine Pioneer uniforms, back issues of Soviet journals, and even, if you're lucky, original propagandist booklets containing the thoughts of Stalin or Brezhnev. *Periniye Liniya Shopping Center, Dumskaya Ulitsa d. 4.* ☎ *8 921 992 0045,* ☎ *812 315 0926. MC, V. Metro: Nevsky Prospect. Map p 92.*

Souvenir Shop NEVSKY PROSPECT   Nothing about this shop differentiates it from any of the others peddling fur hats and matroshkas along Nevsky. Except that this basement was, until as recently as 2005, one of St Petersburg's very few public toilets. *Nevsky Prospect d. 20* ☎ *812 570 1134. MC, V. Metro: Nevsky Prospect. Map p 93.*

Jewelry

Khlebnikov Jewelry Salon NEVSKY PROSPECT   Stunning diamonds, and a deliciously kitsch line in faux military orders. *Nevsky Prospect d. 29/31.* ☎ *812 314 1952.. MC, V. Metro: Gostiny Dvor, Nevsky Prospect. Map p 92.*

Gosting Dvor.

★★★ Northway ANGLIISKAYA NABEREZHNAYA   This must be the most glamorous souvenir store in town, with rococo couches and six-foot chandeliers. Ignore the matrioshkas and balalaikas on the first floor and head downstairs for what seems like miles of Baltic amber. *Angliiskaya Naberezhnaya d. 36.* ☎ *812 312 2062. AE, DC, MC, V. Metro: Gostiny Dvor, Nevsky Prospect. Map p 92.*

Mercury Shop, Grand Hotel Europe NEVSKY PROSPECT   The Mercury Group is Russia's leading luxury retailer, and one of the main drivers of the current retail revolution. This outlet offers Chopard, Fabergé, Mikimoto, and Tiffany. Press your nose up against the bullet-proof glass and just drool. *Grand Hotel Europe, Mikhailovskaya Ul. d. 1/7.* ☎ *812 329 6000. AE, DC, MC, V. Metro: Nevsky Prospect. Map p 93.*

Salon Buré NEVSKY PROSPECT Watchmakers to the discerning since before the Revolution. *Nevsky Prospect d.23.* ☎ *812 571 7534. AE,* *DC, MC, V. Metro: Gostiny Dvor, Nevsky Prospect. Map p 92.*

Yakhont BOLSHAYA MOR-SKAYA   See p 73. *Map p 92.*

Malls, Shopping Centers & Department Stores
Gostiny Dvor NEVSKY PROSPECT Love it or hate it (and it's more than a little tatty and chaotic with much of it currently under refurbishment), this Neoclassical monolith (built in 1757–1785) is the city's oldest shopping mall. *Nevsky Prospect d. 35.* ☎ *812 710 5408. AE, DC, MC, V. Metro: Gostiny Dvor. Map p 92.*

Markets
Art Market NEVSKY PROSPECT A blaze of color in all weathers, the portrait artists, cartoonists, canvasses, and watercolors spill out from the courtyard of the Catholic St Catherine's Cathedral, sometimes as far as Ploshad Ostrovskovo across Nevsky. *Nevsky Prospect d. 32–34. No phone. Rubles only. Metro: Nevsky Prospect. Map p 93.*

Clearing Customs

Most souvenirs can be taken out of the country, but be careful when buying art or antiques. You will need an export permit for any item made more than 50 years ago, and items produced more than 100 years ago are unlikely to be cleared for export.

You will not need an export permit for: contemporary souvenirs, electric samovars, or any books, posters, or reproductions produced within the last 50 years. You may export up to 250g of red caviar: export of black caviar is forbidden.

You will need an export permit for any of these items, regardless of when they were made: icons, paintings (even recent works), carpets and rugs, samovars (not electric samovars).

Most galleries and auction houses will assist in obtaining export clearance: if you need independent advice, contact the Ministry of Culture at Malaya Morskaya Ulitsa d. 17, ☎ 812 117 3496, ☎ 812 3496 5196, ☎ 812 3496 0302. The Customs Service has an advice desk at Pulkovo airport, terminal II (☎ 812 740 2597, ☎ 812 740 2544).

Kuznechny Market VLADIMIR-SKAYA   Recent hostilities haven't yet had too much of an impact on the Georgian and other Caucasian traders here. Expect chaos, haggling, and the best fruit and veg in town. Closed Mon. *Kuznechny Per. d. 3.* ☎ *812 312 4161,* ☎ *812 312 7727. Rubles only. Metro: Vladimir-skaya. Map p 92.*

Udelnaya UDELNAYA   This weekend open-air flea market is a good choice for better priced Soviet memorabilia, fur hats, and antiques. But resist the urge to haggle: the babushkas here need the money more than you do. *Udelnaya metro, no phone. Rubles only. Metro: Udel-naya. Map p 91.*

Bric-a-brac at the Udelnaya flea market.

Vernisazh. See p 15.

Yunona YUNONA It's somewhat cheered up with an antiques market at weekends, but this electronics/bootleg/flea market—apparently bordered by electricity pylons on all sides—is absolutely grim. As an insight into life beyond the façades of the Fontanka, however, it is invaluable. *Prospect Marshala Zhukhova d. 40.* ☎ *812 784 3441,* ☎ *812 747 0200. Rubles only. Metro: Leninsky Prospect, then marshrutki 45, 182, 256, or 339. Map p 92.*

Russian Designers

A Dress GOROKHOVAYA Bright young things, under one roof. *Gorokhovaya Ul. d. 5.* ☎ *812 570 4899. AE, DC, MC, V. Metro: Sennaya Ploshad then trolley bus 17 or various marshrutki to M. Morskaya Ulitsa. Map p 92.*

Liliya Kisselenko SMOLNY One of the founders of the twice-yearly Defile na Neve fashion shows (www.defilenaneve.ru). *Kirochnaya Ul. d. 47.* ☎ *812 271 2552. www.kisselenko.ru. AE, DC, MC, V. Metro: Chernishevskaya. Map p 93.*

A Dress.

Tatiana Parfionova NEVSKY PROSPECT Local girl made good Tatiana Parfionova is one of the few non-Moscow-based designers to have broken into the international fashion scene. *Nevsky Prospect d. 51.* ☎ *812 713 1415,* ☎ *812 713 3668. AE, DC, MC, V. Metro: Mayakovskaya. Map p 92.*

Specialist Food Shops

Kosher Shop ULITSA DEKABRISTOV Kosher foodstuffs, traditional music CDs, and souvenirs. *Lermontovsky Prospect d. 2.* ☎ *812 575 3859,* ☎ *812 575 3857. www.eng.jewishpetersburg.ru. MC, V. Metro: Sadovaya then marshrutka K1. Map p 92.*

Legendi Ararat VLADIMIRSKAYA If you've never tried Armenian cognac, you should. Legendi Ararat is one of the best brands. *Vladimirsky Prospect d. 13/9.* ☎ *812 315 3286. AE, DC, MC, V. Metro: Ligovsky Prospect, Vladimirskaya. Map p 92.*

Supermarkets

Lend Supermarket VLADIMIRSKAYA Less than a supermarket than a gourmet delicatessen, with caviar, *smelt* (a particular kind of local smoked fish), a good range of favorite Western comfort foods, and a staggering range of imported beers. *Vladimirsky Passazh, Vladimirsky Prospect d. 19.* ☎ *812 331 3233. AE, DC, MC, V. Metro: Dostoevskaya, Vladimirskaya. Map p 92.*

Perekriostok CITYWIDE It seems every new mall has a branch of this chain—towards the cheaper end of the market, but an invaluable resource for anyone choosing apartment rentals over hotels. *PIK Mall, Ul. Efimova d. 2.* ☎ *812 336 4790. MC, V. Metro: Sadovaya, Sennaya Ploshad. Map p 92.* ●

5 The Best of the **Outdoors**

Two **Victory Parks**

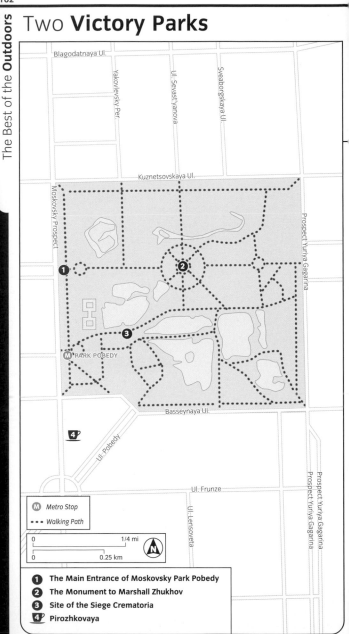

Blagodatnaya Ul.

Yakovlevsky Per.

Ul. Sevastyanova

Sveaborgskaya Ul.

Kuznetsovskaya Ul.

Moskovsky Prospect

Prospect Yuriya Gagarina

1

2

3

M PARK POBEDY

Basseynaya Ul.

4

Ul. Pobedy

Ul. Frunze

Ul. Lensoveta

Prospect Yuriya Gagarina
Prospect Yuriya Gagarina
Prospect Yuriya Gagarina

M Metro Stop

••• Walking Path

| 0 | 1/4 mi |
| 0 | 0.25 km |

N

1 The Main Entrance of Moskovsky Park Pobedy
2 The Monument to Marshall Zhukhov
3 Site of the Siege Crematoria
4 Pirozhkovaya

While both commemorate victory in WWII, St Petersburg's two park pobedy (victory parks) are starkly different. The Primorskoi Park Pobedy, a buzzing fun venue with Russia's best amusement park, is part of the city's northern islands and covered as part of that tour—see p 106. Moskovsky Park Pobedy, however, is an elegant and evocative sanctuary in the midst of the city's most typically Soviet street: there are plans for both parks to be privatized in 2009. Go now, before they lose their Soviet charm. START: **At the main entrance, a short walk north from Park Pobedy metro.**

❶ The Main Entrance of Moskovsky Park Pobedy. While a park was planned on this site as early as 1939, the Siege of Leningrad (see p 50) saw the land (a former brickworks) used instead as mass crematoria for its victims. Most tourists are unaware of the park's tragic history which makes locals uncomfortable. But despite the beer tents and inline skaters, the park does retain an aura of sadness and respect. Opened in July 1946, the inscription above the main entrance says: 'A symbol of undying glory and a living monument to a heroic people.' *Moskovsky Prospect d. 188.* ☎ 812 388 3249, ☎ 812 388 0881.

❷ ★★ The Monument to Marshall Zhukhov. The classic Soviet statuary dotting the park includes this monument to the WWII military leader, erected in 1995 and flanked by Heroes of Socialist Labor and Heroes of the Soviet Union. Two statues near the ponds on either side commemorate

Zoya Kosmodemyanskaya, an 18-year-old partisan executed by the Nazis, the first woman to be (posthumously) made Hero of the Soviet Union, and Alexander Matrosov a 19-year-old soldier awarded the same honor for throwing himself into direct machine-gun fire.

❸ Site of the Siege Crematoria. It's easy to miss, but south of the boat lakes a modest wooden cross marks the site of the former crematoria. The derelict building you will find a few yards south of it hides two more pieces of classic sculpture, *The Front* by Leonid Razumovsky and *The Rear* by Nikolai Gorenyshev.

❹ Pirozhkovaya. A perfect, traditional pirozhkovaya (pie shop) from the stand-up tables to the 1950s tiling and the sweet black tea. On one of the city's most upmarket streets, it's unlikely to remain here for long. Go now. *Moskovsky Prospect d. 192–194. No phone. $.*

Marshall Zhukhov.

Three **Islands**

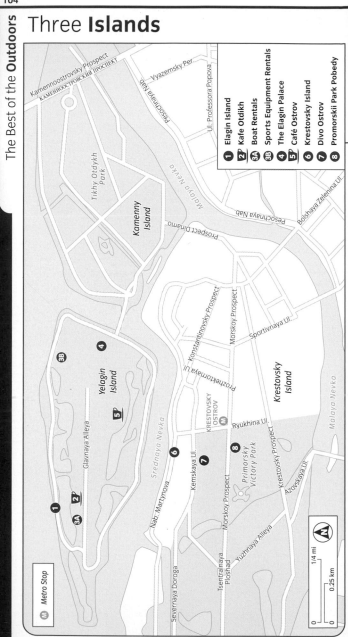

1 Elagin Island
2 Kafe Otdikh
3A Boat Rentals
3B Sports Equipment Rentals
4 The Elagin Palace
5 Café Ostrov
6 Krestovsky Island
7 Divo Ostrov
8 Promorskii Park Pobedy

M Metro Stop

Vyazemsky Per.

Ul. Professora Popova

Kamennoostrovsky Prospect
КАМЕННООСТРОВСКИЙ ПРОСПЕКТ

Peschnaya Nab.

Peschnaya Nab.

Bolshaya Zelenina Ul.

Malaya Nevka

Tikhy Otdykh Park

Kamenny Island

Prospect Dinamo

Morskoy Prospect

Konstantinovsky Prospect

Sportivnaya Ul.

Yelagin Island

Glavnaya Alleya

Prozhektornaya Ul.

KRESTOVSKY OSTROV

Krestovsky Island

Ryukhina Ul.

Srednaya Nevka

Malaya Nevka

Nab. Martynova

Kemskaya Ul.

Primorsky Victory Park

Morskoy Prospect

Krestovsky Prospect

Azovskaya Ul.

Severnaya Doroga

Tsentralnaya Ploshad

Yuzhnaya Alleya

1/4 mi
0.25 km

The three Kirov islands in the Neva Delta hold some of the most stunning parkland in the city. But don't try and cover all three in one day: the transport connections will drive you mad. If you're short of time, Kammeny Island is the one to miss—home to some stunning Style Moderne dachas but, frankly, little else. Instead, this tour takes you from the serenity of Elagin Island's lakes and palaces to the Krestovsky's Victory Park for bike rides, skating and a funfair. **START: At Staraya Derevnya metro, south down Lipovaya Alleya to Primorsky Prospect.**

❶ ★★ **Elagin Island.** Keep your eyes peeled for the tiny slip road that leads to the island over the 3rd Elagin Bridge. For anyone used to the dirt-road-and-debris of most Russian parks, the landscaping in Elagin is breathtaking. *Elagin Park, Elagin Ostrov d. 4.* ☎ *812 430 1130. Admission (weekends and holidays only) 50R adults, 20R students. 6am–midnight summer, 6am–11pm winter.*

❷ **Kafe Otdikh.** A basic park café, but scrupulously clean with real log fires in winter. ☎ *812 430 1861. $.*

❸A **Boat Rentals.** Elagin's lakes and rivers are perfect for beginners, with boat and canoe rentals available west along the bank from Kafe Otdikh. You'll need to leave your passport in addition to a deposit.

Elagin Island.

Boat hire 150R per hour (deposit 1,000R).

❸B **Sports Equipment Rentals.** Heading south from Kafe Otdikh via Glavnaya Alleya will take you to the Yelagin Palace. A more scenic route, however, follows the riverbank, with a series of arrows directing you round one of the palace buildings (and, if you're lucky, past game babushkas going through their paces at the sports club) to the equipment rentals. The website (www.elaginpark.spb.ru—Russian only) promises bikes, skates, and scooters for rent, apparently until 9pm. Don't be too surprised, however, to find it closed much earlier on weekdays. *Rental charges (per hour): inline skates 150R (deposit 2,000R); bikes 150R (deposit 1,500R); children's bikes and scooters 80R (deposit 1,000R).*

4 The Elagin Palace. While under scaffolding as we went to press, the Elagin Palace is a pristine example of Neoclassical architecture, built by Carlo Rossi (1818–1822) for Empress Maria Fedorovna and rebuilt after severe damage in WWII. Several state rooms are open to the public. *Elagin Palace, Elagin Ostrov d. 4.* ☎ *812 430 1131. Excursion prices vary. Closed Mon–Tues.*

5 Café Ostrov. Head south west on any of the paths from Glavnaya Alleya (or follow the signs) to this attractive, modern building complete with outdoor terrace and barbeque—but, again, subject to erratic closing times. ☎ *812 430 053,* ☎ *812 430 0891. $.*

6 Krestovsky Island. From Kafe Ostrov continue south west over a small footbridge to the southernmost edge of the island. From here, the 2nd Elagin Bridge will take you directly to Krestovsky Island. Originally owned by the first Governor of St Petersburg (and Peter I's best friend), Alexander Menshikov, it remained in aristocratic hands until the Revolution.

7 ★★★ kids Divo Ostrov. I would not usually allow any child in my care to set foot in a Russian fairground, but this is different. Scrupulously clean, with some hilarious landscaping (including a flower-covered VW Beetle), a low percentage of beer tents and a large number of young families keep the hooligan element down, even after dark. There's a good selection of traditional rides (and several designed for the very young), as well as thrill rides (including the 75-meter high *Sling-Shot*) for teenagers. *Divo Ostrov,*

Divo Ostrov.

Kemskaya Ul. d. 1a. ☎ *812 323 9705,* ☎ *812 323 9707. www.divo-ostrov. ru. Admission free: see website for ride costs. Tues–Fri 12pm–9pm, Sat–Sun 11am–10pm, closed Mon.*

8 Primorskii Park Pobedy. The second of St Petersburg's victory parks (honoring the naval dead of WWII) was laid out in October 1945 during a massive *Subotnik* or voluntary working Saturday. It's best visited on wheels: pick up a bike or skates from Jet Set at the entrance. The smooth asphalted surface of Morskoi Prospect leads directly to the former Kirov Stadium, due to reopen in 2010 as the new (23.7 billion-ruble) home of Zenit football club. While it's not possible to see the stadium itself, crane your neck for a glimpse of the Kirov statue, in honor of the former Leningrad Party chief, assassinated in 1934. *Primorskii Park Pobedy, Krestovsky Prospect d. 21. See p 105,* **21** *for rentals.* ●

Dining Best Bets

Best Afternoon Tea
Kempinski Hotel Moika
22 $$$ *Nab. Reki
Moiki d. 22* (p 151)

Best Azerbaijani
Baku $$$$$ *Sado-
vaya Ul. d. 23/121*
(p 113)

**Best 'Bizniz'
Lunch**
Bierstube, Corin-
thia Nevskij Palace
Hotel $$$ *Nevsky
Prospect d. 57* (p 150)

Best Blini
★ Rotunda Lounge,
Astoria Hotel, $$$$
Bolshaya Morskaya Ul. d. 39 (p 151)

Best Borscht
★★★ Yolki Palki $$$ *Malaya
Konushennaya Ulitsa d. 9* (p 118)

Best for Breakfast
Dickens $$ *Nab. Reki Fontanki d. 108.*
(p 126)

Best Brunch
L'Europe (Grand Hotel Europe)
$$$$$ *Mikhailovskaya Ul. d. 1/7*
(p 150)

Best on a Budget
★★★ Vostochniy Express $
Ul. Marata d. 21 (p 13)

Best Burger
Stroganoff Steak House $$$$
Konnogvardeisky Bulvar d. 4 (p 117)

Best for Carnivores
★★★ Stroganoff Steak House $$$$
Konnogvardeisky Bulvar d. 4 (p 117)

**Best for a Decent-Cup-of-Coffee-
Without-Having-to-Pay-250-
Rubles-Goddamit**
Mama Roma $$$$$ *Branches
citywide* (p 116)

Afternoon tea in the lounge,
Kempinski Hotel Moika 22.

Best Georgian
★★★ Cat Café $$$
*Stremyannaya Ul.
d. 22/3* (p 114)

Best for Kids
★★★ Stroganoff
Steak House $$$$
*Konnogvardeisky
Bulvar d. 4* (p 117);
and Botanica $$ *Ul.
Pestelya d. 7*
(p 114)

**Best for Midnight
Munchies**
Mama Roma $$$ *Branches
citywide* (p 116)

**Best for Pre-revolu-
tionary Glamour**
The Nobles' Nest $$$$$ *Ul.
Dekabristov d. 21* (p 115)

**Best for a Presidential
Putin-Fest**
★★★ Restoran Podvorye $$$$$
Filtrovskoye Shosse d. 16, Pavlovsk
(p 117)

**Most Surreal Restroom
Experience**
Shury-Mury $$$ Kirochnaya *Ulitsa
d. 3* (p 117)

Best for Soviet Nostalgia
Lenin Zhiv $$ *Nab. Reki Fontanki
d. 4* (p 43)

Best for Vegetarians
★★★ Botanica $$ *Ul. Pestelya d. 7*
(p 114)

Best View
★★★ Gallery Café, Angleterre Hotel
$$ *Malaya Morskaya Ulitsa d. 24*
(p 146); and Bellevue Restaurant,
Kempinski Hotel Moika 22 $$$$$
Reki Moiki d. 22 (p 151)

The Northern Islands **Dining**

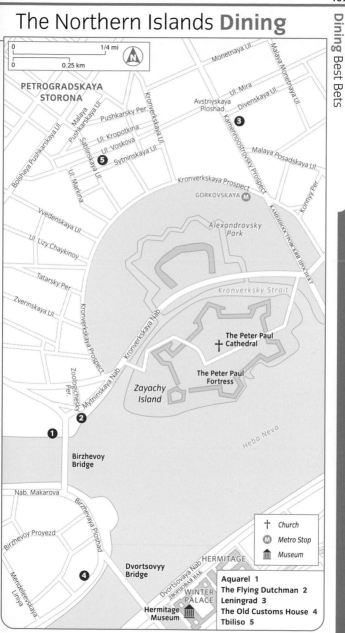

PETROGRADSKAYA STORONA

Monetnaya Ul.
Malaya Monetnaya Ul.
Ul. Mira
Avstriyskaya Ploshad
Divenskaya Ul.
Kronverkskaya Ul.
Pushkarsky Per.
Malaya Pushkarskaya Ul.
Bolshaya Pushkarskaya Ul.
Ul. Kropotkina
Ul. Voskova
Sablinskaya Ul.
Sytninskaya Ul.
Ul. Markina
Malaya Posadskaya Ul.
Kamennoostrovskiy Prospect
Konnyy Per.
Vvedenskaya Ul.
Kronverkskaya Prospect
GORKOVSKAYA Ⓜ
КАМЕННООСТРОВСКИЙ ПРОСПЕКТ
Ul. Lizy Chaykinoy
Alexandrovsky Park
Tatarsky Per.
Zverinskaya Ul.
Kronverksky Strait
Kronverkskaya Prospect
Kronverkskaya Nab.
Zoologichesky Per.
Mytninskaya Nab.
The Peter Paul
✝ Cathedral
The Peter Paul Fortress
Zayachy Island
Heba Nevo
Birzhevoy Bridge
Nab. Makarova
Birzhevaya Ploshad
Birzhevoy Proyezd
Mendeleevskaya Liniya
Dvortsovyy Bridge
Dvortsovaya Nab.
ДВОРЦОВАЯ НАБ.
HERMITAGE
WINTER PALACE
Hermitage Museum 🏛

| 0 | 1/4 mi |
| 0 | 0.25 km |

✝ Church
Ⓜ Metro Stop
🏛 Museum

Aquarel 1
The Flying Dutchman 2
Leningrad 3
The Old Customs House 4
Tbiliso 5

The Best Dining

West of Nevsky **Dining**

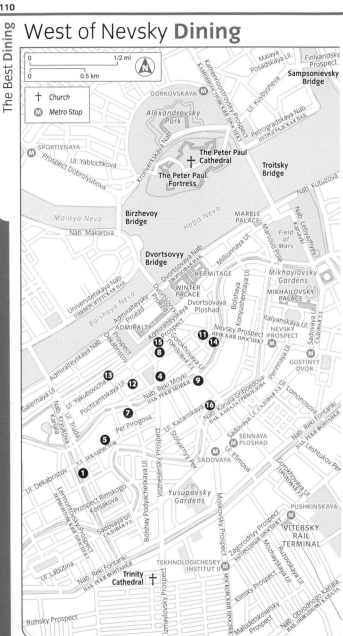

Church †

Metro Stop Ⓜ

0 — 1/2 mi
0 — 0.5 km

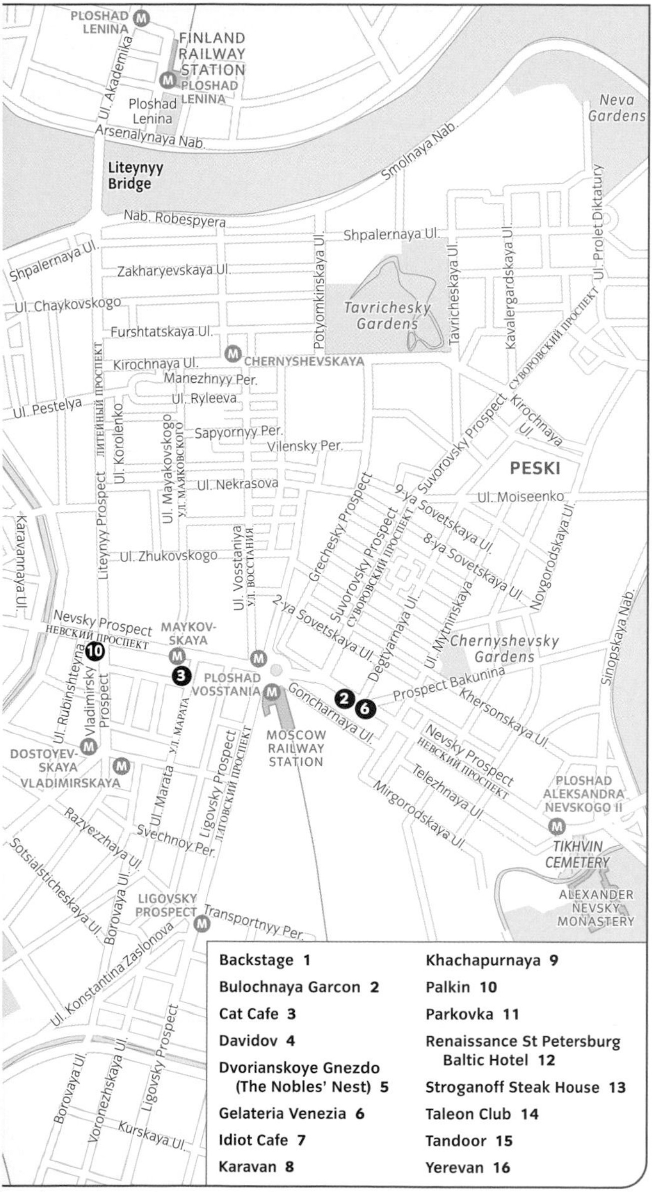

PLOSHAD LENINA Ⓜ
FINLAND RAILWAY STATION
Ⓜ PLOSHAD LENINA
Ul. Akademika
Ploshad Lenina
Arsenalynaya Nab.
Neva Gardens

Liteynyy Bridge

Nab. Robespyera
Shpalernaya Ul.
Shpalernaya Ul.
Zakharyevskaya Ul.
Ul. Chaykovskogo
Furshtatskaya Ul.
Tavrichesky Gardens
Kirochnaya Ul. Ⓜ CHERNYSHEVSKAYA
Manezhnyy Per.
Ul. Ryleeva
Ul. Pestelya
Sapyornyy Per.
Vilensky Per.
Ul. Nekrasova
PESKI
Ul. Moiseenko
Ul. Zhukovskogo
9-ya Sovetskaya Ul.
8-ya Sovetskaya Ul.
Novgorodskaya Ul.
2-ya Sovetskaya Ul.
Chernyshevsky Gardens
Nevsky Prospect НЕВСКИЙ ПРОСПЕКТ
MAYKOV-SKAYA
Ⓜ
Prospect Bakunina
Khersonskaya Ul.
⑩
❸
PLOSHAD VOSSTANIYA Ⓜ
Goncharnaya Ul.
❷❻
Nevsky Prospect НЕВСКИЙ ПРОСПЕКТ
DOSTOYEV-SKAYA Ⓜ
VLADIMIRSKAYA
MOSCOW RAILWAY STATION
Telezhnaya Ul.
PLOSHAD ALEKSANDRA NEVSKOGO II Ⓜ
Razvezzhaya Ul.
Mirgorodskaya Ul.
TIKHVIN CEMETERY
Svechnoy Per.
LIGOVSKY PROSPECT Ⓜ
Transportnyy Per.
ALEXANDER NEVSKY MONASTERY
Ul. Konstantina Zaslonova
Kurskaya Ul.

Backstage **1**	Khachapurnaya **9**
Bulochnaya Garcon **2**	Palkin **10**
Cat Cafe **3**	Parkovka **11**
Davidov **4**	Renaissance St Petersburg Baltic Hotel **12**
Dvorianskoye Gnezdo (The Nobles' Nest) **5**	Stroganoff Steak House **13**
Gelateria Venezia **6**	Taleon Club **14**
Idiot Cafe **7**	Tandoor **15**
Karavan **8**	Yerevan **16**

East of Nevsky **Dining**

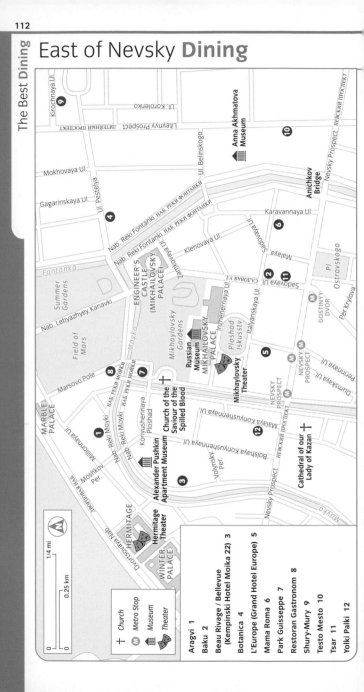

Aragvi 1
Baku 2
Beau Rivage / Bellevue
(Kempinski Hotel Moika 22) 3
Botanica 4
L'Europe (Grand Hotel Europe) 5
Mama Roma 6
Park Guisseppe 7
Restoran Gastronom 8
Shury-Mury 9
Testo Mesto 10
Tsar 11
Yolki Palki 12

★★★ **Aragvi** FONTANKA *GEOR-GIAN* Desultory service, but out-standing food. Go for a selection of starters including *pikali* (spinach with walnuts), *baklazhani* (auber-gines stuffed with walnuts and cream), *sitsivi* (chicken in spicy nut sauce), and *khachapuri* (cheese-stuffed soft dough bread). Portions are massive, but they're happy to pack up a doggy bag to take away. *Nab. Reki Moiki d. 9.* ☎ *812 570 5643. Entrees 240R–480R. AE, V. Lunch and dinner daily. Metro: Nevsky Prospect. Map p 112.*

Aquarel PETROGRADSKAYA *FUSION* While some claim it's now past its best, this was once one of the most elegant and upmarket Euro-Asian fusion venues. Still rec-ommended, nonetheless, for the stella Strelka views from its Neva bank mooring. Find cheaper options in the Aquarelissimo café on the floor above. *Prospect Dobrolyubova d. 14a.* ☎ *812 320 8600 Entrees 550-1300R. MC, V. Lunch & dinner daily. Metro: Sportivnaya. Map p 109.*

Backstage TEATRALNAYA PLO-SHAD CUISINE Reliable stalwart before a visit to the Mariinsky.

Teatralnaya Ploshad d. 18/10. ☎ *812 327 0521. Entrees 650R–1,100 R. AE, DC, MC, V. Lunch and dinner daily. Metro: Sadovaya. Map p 110.*

Baku NEVSKY PROSPECT *AZERBAI-JANI/CAUCASIAN* Single women dining alone can still get a bit of a rough deal in Russia—dumped beside the restrooms or forced to wait 45 minutes for food to arrive. This, alas, is one such venue. Included, however, on the strength of (male) friends who insist its kitsch Arabian Nights décor and menu make it an absolute hoot. Watch out for testicles and other offal, and read p 114 (What Not to Eat) before you go. *Sadovaya Ul. d. 12/23.* ☎ *812 571 8470. Entrees 350-2,000R. MC, V. Lunch and dinner daily. Metro: Gostiny Dvor. Map p 112.*

Beau Rivage/Bellevue (Kem-pinski Hotel Moika 22) NEVSKY PROSPECT *FRENCH/EUROPEAN* Classic French cuisine with stunning city views. Wine lovers should also drop in on its 1853 Wine Cellar, and Brits and traditionalists can head for cucumber sandwiches and cakes in the Tea Room. *Nab. Reki Moiki d. 22.* ☎ *812 335 9111. AE, DC, MC, V. Breakfast and dinner daily (Beau*

View over the city from the panoramic Bellevue restaurant on the 9th floor of the Kempinski Hotel Moika 22.

What Not to Eat

St Petersburg's restaurants now offer a choice unthinkable 10 years ago. Not all of it is worth paying for, however. While there are some outstanding restaurants at the top and bottom of the market, mid-range venues—particularly the international offerings (French, Italian, Chinese, Thai)—can be seriously disappointing for the prices charged. When you've had your fill of the Russian staples, do what the locals do and head for the long-established Caucasian eateries. Menus aren't always available in English, so here's what you need to know:

Kutabi (кутабш): thin, crepe-like bread filled with meat, herbs, or cheese. **Kharcho** (харчо): spicy beef soup. **Khachapuri** (хачапури): oven-baked flatbread with cheese. **Khashi** (хаши): be careful here, it's a meat stew, made mainly from pig's trotters and offal; unbelievably, it's traditionally a breakfast dish. **Khinkali** (хинкапи): meat-filled dumplings. **Lobio** (побио): a side dish of kidney beans. **Lyulya** (піопя) kebab: minced beef with herbs and spices. **Kazy** (казш): another one to watch out for, horsemeat sausage. **Manty** (мантш): meat-filled dumplings but note, the texture is closer to pasta than to dough. **Piti** (пити): a slow-cooked stew with lamb and chickpeas. **Satsivi** (сачиви): chicken in a spicy sour cream and walnut sauce: if you try only one Georgian dish, make it this one.

Rivage), entrees 1,750R–2,250R. Breakfast, lunch and dinner daily (Bellevue), entrees 700R–1,500R. Metro: Gostiny Dvor, Nevsky Prospect. Map p 112.

★★★ **kids** **Botanica** LITEINY PROSPECT *VEGETARIAN* Hard to say what is the best feature of this small vegetarian café: the elegant Stalinist building, the dedicated children's room, their clear appreciation of how to make a decent cup of tea, or the super-thin blini. *Ul. Pestelya d. 7.* ☎ *812 727 7091. Entrees 250R–400R. MC, V. Lunch and dinner daily. Metro: Chernishevskaya. Map p 112.*

Bulochnaya Garcon NEVSKY PROSPECT *FRENCH* A cheap, quality snack stop at the top of Nevsky, with quiches and snacks from 100 rubles. Avoid the nearby sister restaurant, however: 225 rubles for a

very basic café au lait? *Nevsky Prospect d. 103.* ☎ *812 717 0728. Entrees 100R–150R. MC, V. Breakfast, lunch and dinner daily. Metro: Ploshad Vosstaniya. Map p 110.*

★★★ **Cat Cafe** VLADIMIRSKAYA *GEORGIAN* Head and shoulders above every other Georgian in the city. A popular spot with local celebs (and absolutely tiny), book in advance or you just won't get in. *Stremyannaya Ul. d. 22/3.* ☎ *812 571 3377. Entrees 300R–500R. MC, V. Lunch and dinner daily. Metro: Mayakovskaya. Map p 110.*

Davidov ST ISAAC'S SQUARE *RUSSIAN* Try the 3,220-ruble 'Russian Table' for the perfect introduction to traditional cooking. Served with beer and a free shot of premium vodka, or Russian 'champanskoye'. *Hotel Astoria, B. Morskaya Ul. d. 39.* ☎ *812 494 5815. AE, DC, MC, V. Lunch and dinner* daily. Metro: Gostiny Dvor, Nevsky Prospect. Map p 110.

Dvorianskoye Gnezdo (The Nobles' Nest) PLOSHAD DEKA-

BRISTOV *RUSSIAN* Serving classic Russian dishes (including beluga, sturgeon, and sautéd bear), this restaurant in the Garden Pavilion of the Yusupov Palace has served George and Barbara Bush, Gerhard Schroeder, and Jacques Chirac. *Ul. Dekabristov d. 21.* ☎ *812 312 0911. Entrees 870R–2,300R. AE, DC, MC, V. Lunch and dinner daily. Metro: Sadovaya. Map p 110.*

The Flying Dutchman PETRO-

GRADSKAYA *INTERNATIONAL* Probably a venue for the young and fashionable rather than gourmets, and possibly trying just a little bit too hard: a restaurant-nightclub-gym? On a boat? *Mutninskaya Nab. d. 6.* ☎ *812 336 3737. Entrees 500RUB–1,500RUB. MC, V. Lunch & dinner daily. Metro: Sportivnaya. Map p 109.*

Gelateria Venezia PLOSHAD

VOSTANNIYA *ITALIAN* Homemade Italian ice cream in a faux Italianate interior. Also panini and pasta. *Nevsky Prospect d. 107.* ☎ *8 906 279 0346. Entrees from 200R. MC, V. Lunch and dinner daily. Metro: Ploshad Vostanniya. Map p 110.*

Idiot Cafe FONTANKA *VEGETAR-

IAN* The best known of the city's (few) vegetarian restaurants, worth a visit for meat-eaters for cheap and filling breakfasts and a relaxing Russian-intelligentsia-apartment interior. *Nab. Reki Moiki d. 82.* ☎ *812 315 1675. Entrees 200R–1,100R. MC, V. Breakfast, lunch and dinner daily. Metro: Sadovaya. Map p 110.*

★★ Karavan FONTANKA *CAUCA-

SIAN* Very much a business dining venue, but prices are surprisingly reasonable and the Central Asian/Caucasian dishes are perfectly done. *Vosnesensky Prospect d. 46.*

☎ *812 310 5678. Entrees 200R–900R. MC, V. Lunch and dinner daily. Metro: Sadovaya. Map p 110.*

Khachapurnaya CITYWIDE *GEOR-

GIAN* *Khachapuri* is a traditional Georgian soft-dough bread, usually filled with cheese and herbs. This chain sells them throughout the city, together with traditional Georgian staples. Very popular with the lunchtime office crowd, you might need to go early or late to be sure of a table. *Gorokhovaya Ul. d. 17.* ☎ *812 315 4542. Entrees 190R–300R. Rubles only. Lunch and dinner daily. Metro: Sadovaya, Sennaya Ploshad. Map p 110.*

L'Europe (Grand Hotel Europe) NEVSKY PROSPECT *EURO-

PEAN* Exquisite food in a flawlessly restored Art Nouveau interior, complete with stained glass ceiling, paneled gallery and floor-to-ceiling stained glass mural. The food here is French/European, but you'll find Russian specialties in the Caviar Bar next door. Worth living on *kasha* (buckwheat porridge) all week to splurge on the 3,950-ruble Sunday brunch. *Mikhailovskaya Ul. d. 1/7.* ☎ *812 329 6000. Entrees 1,450R–3,200R. AE, DC, MC, V. Breakfast,*

Davidov, Hotel Astoria.

lunch and dinner daily. Metro: Nevsky Prospect., Gostiny Dvor. Map p 112.

Leningrad PETROGRADSKAYA *RUSSIAN* Superbly elegant venue (a former factory, a stone's throw from the Lenfilm studios) and as painfully hip as you would expect from the founder of Decadance nightclub. The dedicated "New Russian" menu really says it all. *Kamennoostrovsky Prospect d. 11a.* ☎ *812 644 4446. Entrees 390RUB–1350RUB. MC, V. Lunch & dinner daily. Metro: Petrogradskaya, Gorkovskaya. Map p 109.*

★★★ Mama Roma CITYWIDE *ITALIAN* Perfect pizza, an all-you-can-eat salad bar (with proper antipasti), decent coffee, and reasonable wine. And you'll still have change from $30. *Karavannaya Ulitsa d. 3/35.* ☎ *812 314 0347. Entrees 210R–770R. MC, V. Lunch and dinner daily. Metro: Nevsky Prospect, Gostiny Dvor. Map p 112.*

★★★ The Old Customs House VASILIEVSKY ISLAND *FRENCH-RUSSIAN* Consistently ranked as one of the city's (few) venues for real fine dining. *Tamozhenny Per. d. 1.* ☎ *812 327 8980. Entrees 1,000-1,500RUB. MC, V. Lunch & dinner*

Sunday brunch at L'Europe.

daily. Metro:Vasileostrovskaya. Map p 109.

Palkin NEVSKY PROSPECT *RUSSIAN/ EUROPEAN* The history of the Palkin family's Petersburg taverns can be traced back to 1785. This venue, opened in 1875, has hosted Chekhov, Dostoevsky, Gogol, and Tchaikovsky. Converted into a cinema after the Revolution, and a casino in the early 1990s, the main halls of the original restaurant were meticulously restored for its reopening in 2002. Some may find its luxury oppressive, but the quality of the cooking is beyond dispute. *Nevsky Prospect d. 47.* ☎ *812 703 5371. Entrees 940R–1,480R. AE, DC, MC, V. Lunch and dinner daily. Metro: Mayakovskaya. Map p 110.*

Park Guisseppe GRIBOEDOV CANAL *ITALIAN* The food's good and the prices eminently reasonable. But the single most striking thing about this venue is its sheer picture-box prettiness, surrounded by the Mikhailovsky Gardens. *Kanal Griboedova d. 2.* ☎ *812 571 7309. Entrees 240R–960R. MC, V. Lunch and dinner daily. Metro: Gostiny Dvor, Nevsky Prospect. Map p 112.*

★★ Parkovka NEVSKY PROSPECT *RUSSIAN* A somewhat limited menu and packed at peak times, but who could argue with free wine, beer, and as much Movenpick ice cream as you can eat? Be warned though, the one hour limit is strictly enforced: even five minutes over and you'll be charged another 350 rubles. Each! *Nevsky Prospect d. 13/9.* ☎ *812 315 1558. Entrees 350R. Rubles only. Lunch and dinner daily. Metro: Nevsky Prospect. Map p 110.*

★★ Renaissance St Petersburg Baltic Hotel ST ISAAC'S SQUARE *INTERNATIONAL* Some swear by the breakfast buffet, others by their burgers, others by the views from the sixth-floor Terrace Bar (see p 126). But what does it for me is their highly commendable three-in-one approach to puddings: order the 'trio' desserts with coffee in the T Lounge (lobby bar) and get a mini crème bruleé, tiramisu and chocolate mousse. *Pochtamtskaya Ul. d. 4.* ☎ *812 380 4000. AE, DC, MC, V. Breakfast, lunch and dinner daily. Metro: Nevsky Prospect, then marshrutka K22, K323. Map p 110.*

Restoran Gastronom GRIBOE-DOV CANAL *EUROPEAN* With a fabulous summer verandah directly opposite the Field of Mars, this offers reasonably priced and per-fectly cooked main courses, as well as rationally priced tea and coffee (from 70 rubles a cup). *Nab. Reki Moiki d. 1/7.* ☎ *812 314 3849. Entrees 250R–450R. MC, V. Lunch and dinner daily. Metro: Gostiny Dvor, Nevsky Prospect. Map p 112.*

Shury-Mury LITEINY PROSPECT *RUSSIAN/CAUCASIAN* Do not be put off by the minimalist/oriental décor. The food here is fresh, hot, well pre-pared, and cheap, with many Central Asian and Russian staples. Although the floor to ceiling mirrors in the rest room are somewhat unnerving. *Kirochnaya Ul. d. 3.* ☎ *812 272 7377. Entrees 200R–450R. MC, V. Lunch and dinner daily. Metro: Chernishevskaya. Map p 112.*

★★★ kids Stroganoff Steak House ST ISAAC'S SQUARE *INTER-NATIONAL* Outstanding. Imported Australian meats, reasonably priced international wines (from 600 rubles a bottle), plus a dedicated no smoking hall and children's playroom. Portions are massive: think hard before order-ing a starter. *Konnogvardiesky Blv. d. 4.* ☎ *812 314 5514. Entrees 490R–1,450R. Business lunches from 340R. AE, DC, MC, V. Lunch and dinner daily. Metro: Nevsky Prospect then trolley*

bus 5 or 22, marshrutka K22, K323. Map p 110.

Taleon Club NEVSKY PROSPECT *EUROPEAN/RUSSIAN* In the former Yeliseev mansion, now a multi-restaurant-casino-bar complex, the wine list at the flagship Taleon Restaurant tells you everything you need to know: Chateau Lafit Roth-schild, Chateau Margaux, Chateau Petrus etc. etc.. Splurge on the 3,100-ruble Sunday brunch, or go for the very democratic 1,000-ruble weekday business lunch menu. *Nab. Reki Moiki d. 59.* ☎ *812 324 9911. Entrees 1,225R–3,700R. MC, V. Lunch and dinner daily. Metro: Nevsky Prospect. Map p 110.*

Tandoor ADMIRALTISKAYA *INDIAN* As Indian restaurants go this isn't entirely authentic; Brits, in particu-lar, will raise an eyebrow at the chopped carrots in the Tikka Masala. But it is a cheap spice fix and the portions are massive: per-fect for a night on the beer. *Vosne-sensky Prospect d. 2.* ☎ *812 312 3886. Entrees 350R–700R (set dinner 750R). MC, V. Lunch and dinner daily. Metro: Nevsky Prospect, Sado-vaya. Map p 110.*

Tbiliso PETROGRADSKAYA *GEOR-GIAN* Not the most attractive loca-tion, directly behind the Sytinsky market, but offering consistently good, moderately priced Georgian specialities. The shashlik (kebabs) are a must-try. *Sytninskaya Ul. d. 10.* ☎ *812 232 9391. Entrees 210RUB–680RUB. MC, V. Lunch & dinner daily. Metro: Petrogradskaya. Map p 109.*

★★★ Testo Mesto LITEINY PROS-PECT *RUSSIAN* The city's best *pirozhkovaya* (pie shop). Massive portions, bargain-basement prices and management that takes food quality very seriously indeed: all water on the premises is filtered five

Best of the Buffets

Eating in St Petersburg can be hard on the wallet, particularly for families. If you can't stand McDonald's or yet another *salat stolichny* at Yolki Palki, head for the weekday buffet lunches at the Western hotels. The Holiday Club St Petersburg's **Sevilla Restaurant** must be the city's best kept secret, offering soup, salads (including delicious antipasti), hot dishes, desserts, water, and coffee for a bargain 595 rubles. It's quite standard corporate catering fodder, but the Novotel's **Coté Jardin** serves up an impressive range of salads, soup, hot dishes, and desserts for 600 rubles. It's open until 4pm, so dodge the queues with a late lunch. But the **Bierstube** at the Corinthia Nevskij Palace Hotel (880R) has to be the best of the bunch: antipasti, smoked meats, salads, delicious main courses, and the best dessert selection by quite some margin. *Holiday Club St Petersburg, Birzhevoi Per. d. 24.* ☎ *812 335 2200. Novotel St Petersburg, Ul. Mayakovskogo d. 3a.* ☎ *812 335 1188. Corinthia Nevskij Palace Hotel St Petersburg, Nevsky Prospect d. 57.* ☎ *812 380 2001.*

times before it reaches your cup. *Liteiny Prospect d. 57.* ☎ *579 8757. Pie portions start at 36R. Rubles only. Breakfast, lunch and dinner daily. Metro: Mayakovskaya. Map p 112.*

Tsar NEVSKY PROSPECT *RUSSIAN* A new offering from Ginza Project (the people behind super cool venues Tiffany's Café, Jelsomino etc.) opened September 2008. *Sadovaya Ul. d. 12.* ☎ *812 640 1900. Entrees 380R–1,450R. MC, V. Lunch and dinner daily. Metro: Gostiny Dvor. Map p 112.*

Yolki Palki CITYWIDE *RUSSIAN* The country-dacha décor's over the top and they overdo it on the mayonnaise: but this chain is a bargain

belly-filler for tourists, and the borscht is as good as you'll find in any *elitny* restaurant. *M. Konushennaya Ul. d. 9.* ☎ *812 571 0385. Entrees 145R–490R. MC, V. Lunch and dinner daily, this branch 24hr. Metro: Nevsky Prospect. Map p 112.*

★★★ **Yerevan** FONTANKA *ARMENIAN* Traditional dishes, perfectly cooked, in an unpretentious, reasonably priced venue. Try the *kyufta* (beef with cognac and onion), the *tolma* (minced lamb in vine leaves), and the Kotaik beer, a local Armenian brew. *Nab. Reki Fontanki d. 51.* ☎ *812 703 3821. Entrees 320R–1,120R. MC, V. Lunch and dinner daily. Metro: Gostiny Dvor. Map p 110.* ●

Nightlife Best Bets

Best for Bachelors
Rossis *Ulitsa Zodchevo Rossi d. 1/3* *(p 125)*

Best Bar
★★★ Lobby Bar, Grand Hotel Europe *Mikhailovskaya Ulitsa d. 1/7* *(p 125)*

Most Beautiful Boozer
★★★ Ryumochnaya (Vodka Room No. 1), *Konnogvardeisky Bulvar d. 4* *(p 126)*

Best for Beer
Tinkoff $$$ *Kazanskaya Ulitsa d. 7* *(p 127)*

Best for Blues
Jimi Hendrix Blues Club *Liteiny Prospect d. 33 (p 128)*

Best for a Boogie
Money Honey, *Apraskin Dvor d. 14* *(p 128)*

Best for Couples
Terrace Bar (Renaissance St Petersburg Baltic Hotel) *Pochtamskaya Ulitsa d. 4.* *(p 126)*

Best Hookahs
★★★ Chainy Dom, *Ulitsa Rubensteina d. 24 (p 125)*

Best for Jazz
JFC Jazz Club *Shpalernaya Ulitsa d. 33 (p 128)*

Best Pub
★★★ Dickens *Nab. Reki Moiki d. 108 (p 126)*

Best for Soviet Nostalgia
★★★ Chet Poberi! *Sadovaya Ulitsa d. 28/30 (p 126)*

Best for Spinning Discs While You Spin-Dry Your Smalls
Kafe Stirka 40, *Kazanskaya Ulitsa d. 26 (p 127)*

Best for Under-30 Clubbers
Griboedov, *Voronezhskaya Ulitsa d. 2a (p 127)*

The Lobby Bar on the Grand Hotel Europe.

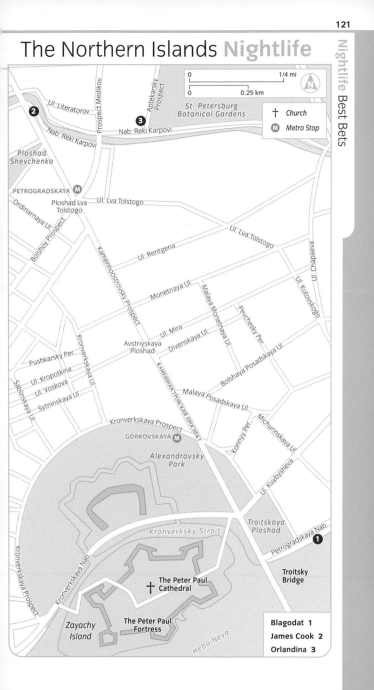

The Northern Islands Nightlife

Ul. Literatorov

Prospect Medikov

Aptekarsky Prospect

St. Petersburg Botanical Gardens

Nab. Reki Karpovi

Nab. Reki Karpova

Ploshad Shevchenko

† Church

Ⓜ Metro Stop

PETROGRADSKAYA Ⓜ

Ploshad Lva Tolstogo

Ul. Lva Tolstogo

Ordinarnaya Ul.

Bolshoy Prospect

Ul. Lva Tolstogo

Ul. Chapaeva

Ul. Rentgena

Ul. Kotovstogo

Kamennoostrovsky Prospect

Monetnaya Ul.

Malaya Monetnaya Ul.

Pevchesky Per.

Ul. Mira

Avstriyskaya Ploshad

Divenskaya Ul.

Bolshaya Posadskaya Ul.

Pushkarsky Per.

Kronverkskaya Ul.

Ul. Kropotkina

Ul. Voskova

Sablinskaya Ul.

Sytninskaya Ul.

Kamennostrovskiy prospekt

Malaya Posadskaya Ul.

Kronverkskaya Prospect

GORKOVSKAYA Ⓜ

Alexandrovsky Park

Konnyy Per.

Michurinskaya Ul.

Ul. Kuybysheva

Troitskaya Ploshad

Kronverksky Strait

Petrogradskaya Nab.

Kronverkskaya Nab.

The Peter Paul † Cathedral

Troitsky Bridge

Kronverkskaya Prospect

Zayachy Island

The Peter Paul Fortress

Reba Neva

Blagodat 1

James Cook 2

Orlandina 3

West of Nevsky Nightlife

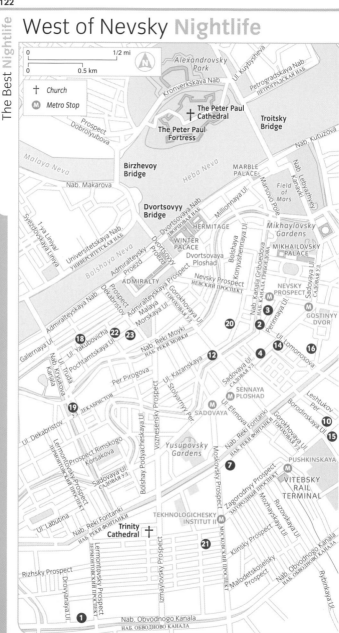

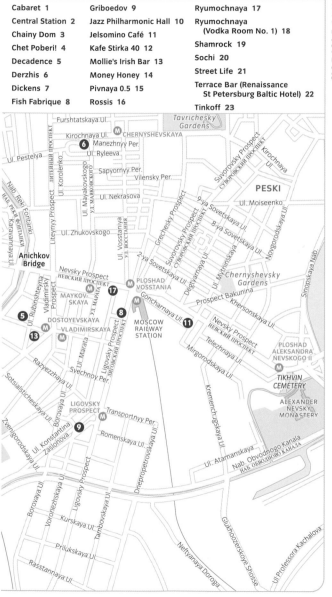

East of Nevsky Nightlife

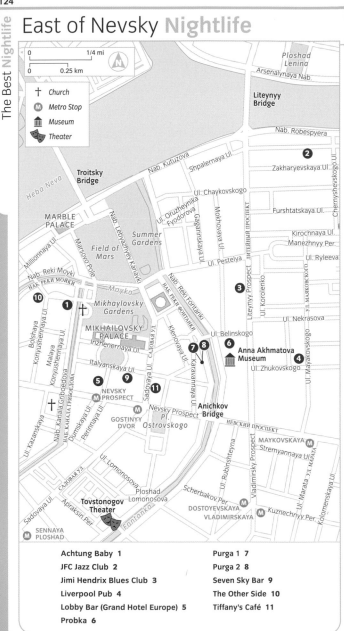

Achtung Baby 1
JFC Jazz Club 2
Jimi Hendrix Blues Club 3
Liverpool Pub 4
Lobby Bar (Grand Hotel Europe) 5
Probka 6

Purga 1 7
Purga 2 8
Seven Sky Bar 9
The Other Side 10
Tiffany's Café 11

Bars

★★★ Chainy Dom VLADIMIR-SKAYA   It's thick with hookah smoke after about 8pm, but this must be one of the most unpretentious, relaxing, and exotic bars in the city. Tiny gold bells to summon a waiter, a piece of poetry to take away with your bill, cocktails to knock you senseless and fruit cocktails so thick you'll need to eat them with a spoon. *Ul. Rubensteina d. 24.* ☎ *812 671 2784. Metro: Dostoevskaya, Mayakovskaya. Dumskaya Ul. d. 5/22.* ☎ *812 314 8417. No cover. Metro: Gostiny Dvor. Map p 122.*

Decadence VLADIMIRSKAYA Petersburgers, in general, have a healthily low threshold for the 'face control' and other nonsense so prevalent in the capital. Not here. A venue in which to see and be seen (or, more likely, turned away from). Wed–Sat only. *Sherbakov Per. d. 17.* ☎ *812 947 7070. Cover varies. Fri–Sat only. Metro: Dostoevskaya. Map p 122.*

Derzhis CHERNISHEVSKAYA A cocktail list running into the hundreds. *Ul. Mayakovskovo d. 56.* ☎ *812 272 0970. No cover. Metro: Chernishevskaya. Map p 122.*

Jelsomino Café PLOSHAD VOSSTANIYA   Super swanky 'New Russian' DJ bar with karaoke. *Poltavskaya Ul. d. 5/29.* ☎ *812 703 5796. No cover. Metro: Ploshad Vosstaniya. Map p 122.*

★★★ Lobby Bar (Grand Hotel Europe) NEVSKY PROSPECT   A dark, cozy Art Deco interior, cool jazz, and luxurious cocktails. Bliss. *Mikhailovskaya Ul. d. 1/7.* ☎ *812 329 6000. www.grand-hotel-europe. com. No cover. Metro: Nevsky Prospect. Map p 124.*

Seven Sky Bar.

Probka FONTANKA   Wine in Russia tends to be either cheap and nasty or good but extortionate. Not here: Australian imports start at 990 rubles a bottle, with many others available by the glass. *Ul. Belinskovo d. 5.* ☎ *812 273 4904. No cover. Metro: Gostiny Dvor. Map p 124.*

Rossis FONTANKA   Personally I found the queues and security a bit more than I could put up with, but that many international bankers can't be wrong. Although they could just have been out on the pull: the female contingent here being very ditzy and very, very young. *Ul. Zodchevo Rossi d. 1/3.* ☎ *812 710 4016. Cover varies. Metro: Gostiny Dvor. Map p 122.*

Seven Sky Bar NEVSKY PROSPECT   DJ bar on the top floor of the Grand Palace shopping center. Very popular pre-party venue, young crowd. *Italianskaya Ul. d. 15.* ☎ *812 449 9432. www.sevensky bar.ru. No cover. Metro: Gostiny Dvor, Nevsky Prospect. Map p 124.*

Pivnaya 0.5.

Terrace Bar (Renaissance St Petersburg Baltic Hotel)
ST ISAAC'S SQUARE   Panoramic city views from the sixth floor of the Renaissance Hotel, with an elegant outdoor terrace in summer. *Pochtamskaya Ul. d. 4.* ☎ *812 380 4000. www.marriott.com. No cover. Metro: Nevsky Prospect, then marshrutka K22, K323. Map p 122.*

Tiffany's Café NEVSKY PROSPECT
The St Petersburg beau monde: very, very cool, very rich, very exclusive. Go at least once (or try to) if only to see what can be achieved by New Russian design unchecked by any financial (or other) constraints. *Sadovaya Ul. d. 12.* ☎ *812 925 4000. www.tiffanycafe.ru. No cover. Metro: Gostiny Dvor. Map p 124.*

Brew Bars, Pubs & Drinking Dens
★★★ **Chet Poberi!** SADOVAYA
If you're over 30 you're going to feel your age here, but go at least once. The interior is a flawless recreation of a Brezhnev era apartment, complete with retro furniture, old Melodia Soviet-label records, ancient radio sets, and the teen detritus familiar to every former Komsomol

member. *Sadovaya Ul. d. 28/30.* ☎ *812 315 7238. No cover. Metro: Gostiny Dvor. Map p 122.*

★★ **Dickens** FONTANKA   Hugely popular with Russians and expats, who come here for the draft beer, pub grub menu, and sports on widescreen. Legendary breakfasts, available from 8am. *Nab. Reki Fontanki d. 108.* ☎ *812 380 7998. No cover. Metro: Technologichesky Institute. Map p 122.*

James Cook PETROGRADSKAYA
Up-market gastro-pub. *Schvedsky Per. d. 3.* ☎ *812 312 3200, Kamenoostrovsky Prospect d. 45.* ☎ *812 347 6581. No cover. Metro: Nevsky Prospect, Petrogradskaya. Map p 121.*

Mollie's Irish Bar VLADIMIRSKAYA   The first of the Irish pubs: original and best. *Ul. Rubensteina d. 36.* ☎ *812 570 3768. No cover. Metro: Vladimirskaya. Map p 122.*

Pivnaya 0.5 VLADIMIRSKAYA
Super-slick and ultra-chic, a million miles from the pivnayas (beer halls) of old. *Zagorodny Prospect d. 44/2.* ☎ *812 315 1038. No cover. Metro: Pushkinskaya, Vladimirskaya. Map p 122.*

★★ **Ryumochnaya** VLADIMIRSKAYA   In Soviet days a Ryumochnaya was a clip joint selling shots of vodka—most of them, alas, now long gone. Purists will tell you today's models are a pastiche (see below), but the smoke-stained walls, vinyl-topped tables, and nicotine haze all look pretty authentic to me. *Pushkinskaya Ul. d. 1.* ☎ *812 764 7514. No cover. Metro: Mayakovskaya, Ploshad Vosstaniya. Map p 122.*

Ryumochnaya (Vodka Room No. 1) ST ISAAC'S SQUARE   Now this venue is most definitely a pastiche: no Ryumochnaya ever had a soft-lit chandeliered interior like this.

It's so beautifully done, however, it's churlish to complain. Part of the Vodka Museum on Konnogvardeiskaya: buy a 300-ruble *degustinaya* ticket and get three sample shots. *Konnogvardeisky Blv. d. 4.* ☎ *812 570 6420. No cover. Metro: Nevsky Prospect, then trolley bus 5 or 22, marshrutka K22, K323. Map p 122.*

Shamrock TEATRALNAYA PLO-SHAD Widescreen sports and occasional live acts, and, they claim, popular with members of the nearby Mariinsky Theater. *Ul. Deka-bristov d. 27.* ☎ *812 570 4625. www.shamrock.spb.ru. Metro: Sado-vaya, then marshrutka K1, K350, K124, K186. Map p 122.*

Tinkoff GOROKHOVAYA/MOS-KOVSKY PROSPECT Don't be fooled: this brand, founded in 1998 by eponymous entrepreneur Oleg Tinkov, is now owned by Sun Inter-brew, part of drinks giant InBev (owners of Stella Artois, Becks, etc.). The venues, however, remain inde-pendent, offering Russian and West-ern gastropub food, widescreen sports, and beer on draught: includ-ing an 'unlimited' offer for 999 rubles. *Kazanskaya Ulitsa d. 7.* ☎ *812 718 5566 and Varshavskaya Ul. d. 23.* ☎ *812 313 0517. www. tinkoff.ru. No cover. Metro: Nevsky Prospect, Sennaya Ploshad and Moskovskaya, Park Pobedi. Map p 122.*

Clubs

Achtung Baby KONUSHENNAYA PLOSHAD Popular DJ bar and dance venue, young crowd. *Konush-ennaya Ploshad d. 2.* ☎ *No phone. Cover varies. Metro: Nevsky Pros-pect. Map p 124.*

Blagodat PETROGRADSKAYA Perfect kitschy Russian excess: restaurants on three floors (includ-ing a rococo recreation of a theater,

complete with private boxes) and karaoke from 10pm. *Petrovskaya Nab. d. 2.* ☎ *812 327 2508. Cover varies. Metro: Gorkhovskaya, Plo-shad Lenina. Map p 121.*

Fish Fabrique LIGOVSKY In the basement of the Pushkinskaya 10 arts center, which tells you every-thing you need to know: chaotic, alternative, and probably not the first choice for sophisticates. But precisely the alternative club culture that differentiates the city from the rest of the country. *Ligovsky Pros-pect d. 53.* ☎ *812 164 4857. Cover varies. Metro: Ploshad Vostanniya. Map p 122.*

Griboedov LIGOVSKY PROSPECT Notorious underground bunker club (in a former bomb shelter), run by members of local band Dva Samo-leta. Best tried on Wednesdays for the Soviet-retro disco night. *Voron-ezhskaya Ulitsa d. 2A.* ☎ *812 764 4355,* ☎ *812 973 7273. Cover var-ies. Metro: Ligovsky Prospect. Map p 122.*

★★★ **Kafe Stirka 40** SADOVAYA Originally founded as the graduation project of German photographer Anke Nowottne, Stirka is the kind of alternative art club-café-bar that this city does so well. But in a launder-ette. Ask a Russian friend to trans-late their website: too deliciously acerbic to ignore. *Kazanskaya Ul. d. 26.* ☎ *812 314 5371. http://40 gradusov.ru. No cover. Metro: Sen-naya Ploshad, Sadovaya. Map p 122.*

Purga 1 FONTANKA Every night is New Year's Eve: purgatory for some perhaps, but a super-kitsch Russophile blowout here. The fun starts at midnight and goes on into the early hours. *Reki Fontanki d. 11.* ☎ *812 570 5123. Table reservations recommended, 500R–2,000R. Metro: Gostiny Dvor. Map p 124.*

Purga 2 FONTANKA   Or hop next door and celebrate a mock wedding. Closed Mon–Tues. *Reki Fontanki d. 11.* ☎ *812 571 2310. See above. Metro: Gostiny Dvor. Map p 124.*

Sochi GOROKHOVAYA   Dumskaya Ulitsa was, only a short time ago, clubland central, hosting legends such as Fidel, Café Club Che, and Datscha. Now under imminent threat from the developers, Datscha at least lives on in this latest incarnation from owner Anna-Christin Albers. *Kazanskaya Ul. d. 7.* ☎ *812 312 0140,* ☎ *812 952 2594. No cover. Metro: Sadovaya, Nevsky Prospect. Map p 122.*

Gay Clubs

Cabaret BALTISKY VOKZAL   Cited as a gay venue, but pretty much open to all and worth a visit for the transvestite drag shows. *Nab. Obvodnovo Kanala d. 181.* ☎ *812 575 4512. Cover varies. Metro: Baltiyskaya. Map p 122.*

Central Station SADOVAYA   Sister club of the Moscow original, and the key gay venue in town. *Ul. Lomonosova d. 1/28.* ☎ *812 312 3600. Cover varies. Metro: Gostiny Dvor, Nevsky Prospect. Map p 122.*

Jazz & Blues

Jazz Philharmonic Hall VLADIMIRSKAYA   The most formal of the jazz venues, with a heavy 40s–50s bent. *Zagorodny Prospect d. 27.* ☎ *812 764 8565. www.jazz-hall. spb.ru. Cover varies. Metro: Pushkinskaya, Vladimirskaya. Map p 122.*

JFC Jazz Club LITEINY PROSPECT   Said to be the most radical of the main jazz venues, with monthly Ethno World events and blues nights on Mondays. *Shpalernaya Ul. d. 33.* ☎ *812 272 9850. Cover varies. Metro: Chernishevskaya. Map p 124.*

Jimi Hendrix Blues Club LITEINY PROSPECT   The only dedicated blues venue in town. The food is highly rated, the sound system less so. *Liteiny Prospect d. 33.* ☎ *812 579 8813. Cover varies. Metro: Chernishevskaya. Map p 124.*

Street Life MOSKOVSKY PROSPECT   A relatively new opening (on the former site of notorious gay Club 69), said to be giving the established jazz haunts a run for their money. *2nd Krasnoarmeiskaya Ul. d. 6.* ☎ *812 575 0545. Cover varies. Metro: Technologichesky Institute. Map p 122.*

Live Music

Liverpool Pub NEVSKY PROSPECT   The Russian take on Beatlemania. All you need is plov. *Ul. Mayakovskovo d. 16.* ☎ *812 579 2054. www.liverpool.ru. No cover. Metro: Mayakovskaya. Map p 124.*

Money Honey SADOVAYA   St Petersburg's original (only) rockabilly venue. The crowd here is well under 30, but this is a warm, unpretentious club and no one will bat an eyelid at any oldies (or nostalgics) hoping to catch a local live act. *Sadovaya Ul. d. 28 and Apraskin Dvor d. 14.* ☎ *812 310 0549. Cover varies. Metro: Gostiny Dvor. Map p 122.*

Orlandina PETROGRADSKAYA   Long-standing indie venue, with live bands. *Nab. Reki Karpovki d. 5/2.* ☎ *812 234 8046. Cover varies. Metro: Petrogradskaya. Map p 121.*

The Other Side KONUSHENNAYA PLOSHAD   I confess I was underwhelmed, but I suspect I am in the minority. Longstanding expat haunt with live gigs and gastropub menu. *B. Konushennaya Ul. d. 1.* ☎ *812 312 9554. www.theotherside.ru. Cover varies. Metro: Nevsky Prospect. Map p 124.* ●

Arts & Entertainment Best Bets

Best for **Ballet**
Mariinsky Theater, *Teatralnaya Ploshad d. 1. (p 134)*

Best **Banya**
★★★ Holiday Club St Petersburg, *Birzhovoy Pereulok d. 2–4 (p 135)*

Best for the **Big Names**
Ice Palace, *Prospect Pyatiletok d. 1. (p 137)*

Best for **Biking**
★★★ Jet Set, *Primorsky Park Pobedi (p 135)*

Best for **Bladers**
Jet Set, *Primorsky Park Pobedi (p 135)*

Best for **Dicing with Death**
Sosnoborsky Aeroclub, *Kummolovo Airfield (p 139)*

Best for **Ice Skating**
★★★ Moscow Victory Park, *Moskovsky Prospect, Kuznetsovskaya Ulitsa d. 25 (p 138)*

Best for **Kids**
★★★ Oceanarium, *Planet Neptune Shopping Center, Ul. Marata d. 86 (p 139)*

Best for **Men in Tights**
St Petersburg State Male Ballet, *Venues vary (p 134)*

Best for **Swimming**
Neptune Sport & Leisure Complex, *Nab. Obvodnovo Kanala d. 93a (p 140); and Waterville, Pribaltiskaya Hotel, Ul. Korablestroitelei d. 14. (p 140)*

Best for **Swimming with Dolphins**
Dolphinarium, *Konstantinovsky Prospect d. 19 (p 139)*

Mariinsky Theater for ballet.

The Northern Islands **A&E**

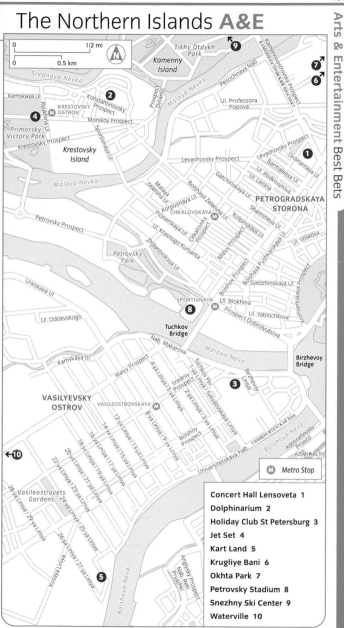

M Metro Stop

Concert Hall Lensoveta **1**
Dolphinarium **2**
Holiday Club St Petersburg **3**
Jet Set **4**
Kart Land **5**
Krugliye Bani **6**
Okhta Park **7**
Petrovsky Stadium **8**
Snezhny Ski Center **9**
Waterville **10**

West of Nevsky **A&E**

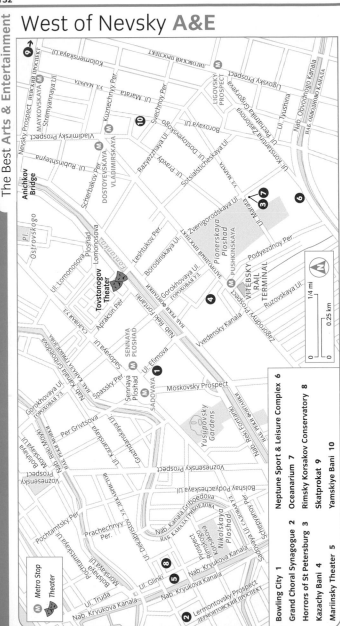

Bowling City 1
Grand Choral Synagogue 2
Horrors of St Petersburg 3
Kazachy Bani 4
Mariinsky Theater 5

Neptune Sport & Leisure Complex 6
Oceanarium 7
Rimsky Korsakov Conservatory 8
Skatprokat 9
Yamskiye Bani 10

East of Nevsky A&E

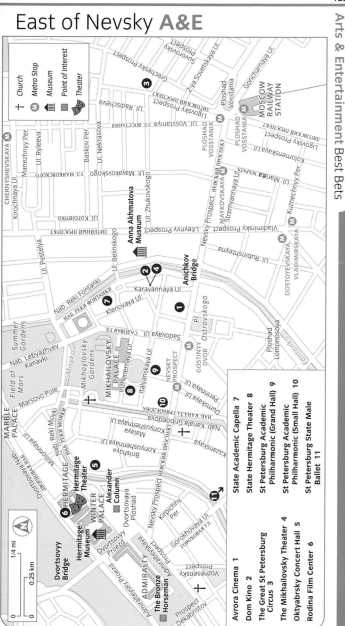

Legend:
+ Church
🅜 Metro Stop
🏛 Museum
⬛ Point of Interest
🎭 Theater

Avrora Cinema 1

Dom Kino 2

The Great St Petersburg Circus 3

The Mikhailovsky Theater 4

Oktyabrsky Concert Hall 5

Rodina Film Center 6

State Academic Capella 7

State Hermitage Theater 8

St Petersburg Academic Philharmonic (Grand Hall) 9

St Petersburg Academic Philharmonic (Small Hall) 10

St Petersburg State Male Ballet 11

1/4 mi

0.25 km

The Southern Outskirts **A&E**

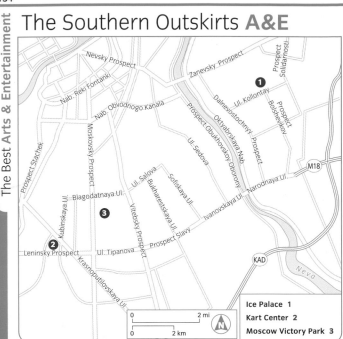

Ice Palace **1**
Kart Center **2**
Moscow Victory Park **3**

St Petersburg **Arts & Entertainment A to Z**

Ballet & Opera

★★★ Mariinsky Theater TEAT-
RALNAYA   Home of the Kirov
Ballet, the Mariinsky is, these days,
equally famous for the work of its
artistic director Valery Gergiev.
Avoid the touts and book online in
advance: their very user-friendly site
also includes plot summaries and
background information on the
major productions, and all in English. *Teatralnaya Ploshad d. 1.*
☎ *812 326 4141. www.mariinsky.
ru. Ticket prices vary. Metro: Sadovaya, Sennaya Ploshad. Map p 132.*

★ State Hermitage Theater
DVORTSOVAYA PLOSHAD   Go, if
only to feast your eyes on Giacomo

Quarenghi's beautiful Neoclassical
auditorium: built in 1785 and painstakingly restored in the 1980s.
Dvortsovaya Nab. d. 34. ☎ *812 579
0226. www.rus-ballet.com. Ticket
prices vary. Metro: Nevsky Prospect.
Map p 133.*

**St Petersburg State Male
Ballet** CITYWIDE   Don't expect the
high camp of the Ballets de Troc:
this is classical ballet at its best.
With no fixed venue of their own,
look out for performances at venues
around town. *Gorokhovaya Ul. d. 71.*
☎ *812 320 0627. Ticket prices and
venues vary. Map p 133.*

The Mikhailovsky Theater

PLOSHAD ISSKUSTV Too often dismissed as the city's second-best venue (despite a 175-year history including premieres of Shostakovich's major works), the controversial appointment of new General Director Vladimir Kekhman has injected new life into the Mikhailovsky, with its 2008 production of *Spartacus*, in particular, touring internationally to considerable acclaim. *Ploshad Isskustv d.1.* ☎ *812 595 4305. www. mikhailovsky.ru. Ticket prices vary. Metro: Nevsky Prospect. Map p 133.*

Banya

★★★ Holiday Club St Petersburg VASILIEVSKY OSTROV Probably not the best choice for purists, but where else are you going to be offered a 'snow sauna' or 'sauna cave'? *Birzhevoi Per. d. 2–4, VSO.* ☎ *812 335 2200. www.holiday clubspa.com. Tickets Mon–Fri 7am–4pm 500R per hour adults, 300R kids; 4pm–11pm and weekends 1,000R per hour adults, 600R kids. Metro: Vasileostrovskaya. Map p 131.*

Kazachy Bani GOROKHOVAYA Super luxurious private banya (for up to 10), open round the clock. *B. Kazachy Per. d. 11.* ☎ *812 712 5079. Banya hire 1,200R per hour. Closed Mon. Metro: Pushkinskaya. Map p 132.*

★★ Krugliye Bani PLOSHAD MUZHESTVA ISome distance from the center, and in one of the city's least attractive neighborhoods, but hugely popular by virtue of its open-air pool. *Karbisheva Ul. d. 29a.* ☎ *812 550 0985,* ☎ *812 297 6409 (Luxe class). Tickets 360R per hour (Luxe), 800R per hour VIP. General class 25R for 90 mins. 8am–10pm, closed Thurs. Metro: Ploshad Muzhestva. Map p 131.*

Yamskiye Bani VLADIMIRSKAYA Actually a full-service fitness center, but also offering individual bani complete with private pool. Dostoevsky and Mussorgsky were regulars, apparently, as well as one Vladimir Ilich Ulyanov (Lenin). *Ul. Dostoevskovo d. 9.* ☎ *812 713 3580. Private banya 600R per hour. 9am–11pm. Metro: Dostoevskaya. Map p 132.*

Biking & Roller-blading

★★★ kids Jet Set CITYWIDE Their Primorski Park Pobedy location is perfect for kids (see p 106), who can skate or ride its full length in complete safety. If you can stand the stares, hire a Segway (two-wheeled stand-on electric transporter) and glide elegantly round to the Divo Ostrov funfair. *Jet Set* ☎ *973 2145. Skate hire 230R–330R per hour adults, 200R kids. Bike hire 250R. Segway hire 550R for 30min. Deposit of 4,000R and passport required. 11am–10pm. Metro: Krestovsky Ostrov. Map p 131.*

Mariinsky Theater.

Skatprokat PLOSHAD VOSSTAN-IYA   Daily and longer rentals: will deliver to your hotel. *Goncharnaya Ul. d. 7.* ☎ *812 717 6838. www. skatprokat.ru. Daily rental from 400R, 6,000R deposit required (3,000R with passport). Metro: Ploshad Vosstaniya. Map p 132.*

Cinema

★★ Avrora Cinema NEVSKY PROSPECT   Russian and international releases and the occasional original-language art film. The real point, however, is its gorgeous 1913 building. *Nevsky Prospect d. 60.* ☎ *812 315 5254 (answerphone, Russian only),* ☎ *812 942 8020 (tickets). Tickets 70R–250R. Metro: Nevsky Prospect. Map p 133.*

Dom Kino NEVSKY PROSPECT Host to the New British Cinema festival every November, this is the city's best bet for non-Russian films. *Karavannaya Ul. d. 12.* ☎ *812 314 5614,* ☎ *812 314 0638 (answerphone Russian only). Tickets 120R–180R. Metro: Gostiny Dvor, Nevsky Prospect. Map p 133.*

Rodina Film Center NEVSKY PROSPECT   Scene of innumerable art film festivals: worth a look for world cinema classics in the Maly (small) Hall. *Karavannaya Ul. d. 12.* ☎ *812 571 6131. Tickets 80R–120R. Metro: Gostiny Dvor, Nevsky Prospect. Map p 133.*

Classical Music
Grand Choral Synagogue
SADOVAYA   Occasional klemzer and cantor concerts. *Lermontovsky Prospect d. 2.* ☎ *812 713 8186. www.eng.jewishpetersburg.ru. Metro: Sadovaya then marshrutka K1. Map p 132.*

Rimsky Korsakov Conservatory
TEATRALNAYA PLOSHAD Opera and ballet from the staff and students of Russia's first music academy (founded in 1862 by its first director, Anton Rubinstein). Competitions and concerts in the Maly Zal provide an opportunity to catch future classical stars. *Teatralnaya Ploshad d. 3.* ☎ *Bolshoi Zal: 812 312 2519,* ☎ *Maly Zal: 812 571 1074,* ☎ *812 571 0506. www. conservatory.ru. Ticket prices for the Bolshoi Zal vary: entrance to the Maly Zal is typically free. Metro: Sennaya Ploshad, then marshrutka 1, 67, 124. Map p 132.*

The Grand Choral Synagogue.

★★ State Academic Capella

PALACE SQUARE   Tracing its origins to Ivan III's Tsar's Servant Choir, founded in 1479, the Capella is now recognized as the country's leading choral ensemble, thanks to former directors including Mikhail Glinka and Nikolai Rismky-Korsakov. *Nab. Reki Moiki.* ☎ 812 314 1058. *Ticket prices vary. Metro: Nevsky Prospect, Gostiny Dvor. Map p 133.*

St Petersburg Academic Philharmonic NEVSKY PROSPECT

A stalwart of the annual Winter Festival, running in the last two weeks of December. Major works in the Grand Hall, chamber orchestras and specialist ensembles in the Small Hall. *Grand Hall, Mikhailovskaya Ul. d. 2.* ☎ 812 312 9871, ☎ 812 710 4085, box office ☎ 812 710 4257. *Small Hall, Nevsky Prospect d. 30.* ☎ 812 312 4585, box office ☎ 812 571 8333. www.saintpetersburg philharmonic.com, www.philharmonia. spb.ru. *Ticket prices vary. Metro: Nevsky Prospect. Map p 133.*

St. Petersburg Academic Philharmonic.

Ice Skating

Ice Palace PROSPECT BOLSHE-VIKOV   Massive indoor complex, but get a Russian-speaking friend to check the website before you go. A

Tickets

The most user-friendly site for English speakers is http://tickit now.com/. It covers the major venues including the Mariinsky, the Hermitage Theater, the Rimsky-Korsakov Conservatory, and the St Petersburg Philharmonic. www.muzbilet.ru is in Russian only, but should give you a good idea of what's happening. Book tickets online, or order by phone on ☎ 812 303 3333. Order through www. bileter.ru (☎ 812 380 8050) and they'll even deliver, as will www. kassir.ru (☎ 812 703 4040). Artis (www.artis.spb.ru) cover a wider range of events with a more cultural bent. Complete the online form and wait for them to call you back ☎ 812 327 2067 (9am–9pm). You might find it simpler just to pop into a Teatralnaya Kassa (**Театральная каса**): you'll find one at Nevsky Prospect d. 42. Tickets for the Mariinsky sell out fast: order before you arrive at www. mariinsky.ru (there's an English-language page for bookings) and pick up tickets from the box office.

Ice Palace.

major training center for future hockey stars, it's often closed for major matches (including the Russian ice hockey championships) as well as big-ticket concerts. *Prospect Pyatiletok d.* ☎ *812 718 66 20. www.newarena.spb.ru. Tickets with skate hire 350R adults, 250R kids under seven; without skate hire 250R adults, 200R kids under seven. Metro: Prospect Bolshevikov. Map p 134.*

★★★ Moscow Victory Park

MOSCOVSKY PROSPECT   The tennis courts here, directly in front of the faded-but-elegant Soviet sports hall are turned into an outdoor rink. *Moscovsky Prospect.* ☎ *812 388 3249. Inline skate hire: 100R per hour, ice skating 100R per hour, skate hire 100R. Deposit 1,000R with passport. Sports center open 12am–10pm, 11am–10pm Sat–Sun. Map p 134.*

Skiing

Okhta Park VSEVOLOZHSKI DISTRICT   Six runs of up to 60 meters. Snow machines and floodlighting keep the slopes open until 10.30pm. *Okhta Park Ski Center, Syargi, Vsevolozhski District, Leningradskaya Oblast.* ☎ *812 718 1870,* ☎ *812 718 1871. Ski lift passes from 450R per hour weekends adults, 250R kids. Metro: Devyatkino, then marshrutka 621. Map p 131.*

Snezhny Ski Center KOROBITSINO   Four runs (of up to 900 meters), ski-lifts, a children's run, an 'Edelweiss extreme run', and a snowboard park. *Snezhny Ski Center, Korobitsino.* ☎ *812 320 7073,* ☎ *8 901 308 6089. www.snegny.ru. Lift passes weekdays 1,000R adults, 750R kids; weekends 1,200R adults, 1,000R kids. Metro: Parnas or Ozerki, then bus K678. Map p 131.*

Spectator Sports & Major Events

Concert Hall Lensoveta PETROGRADSKAYA   Big-name Russian acts and brickies-in-spandex ageing rockers: but a fabulous Stalinist venue in a former *Dom Kultury* (House of Culture). *Kamenoostrovsky Prospect d. 42.* ☎ *812 346 0438,* ☎ *812 346 3063. Ticket prices vary. Metro: Petrogradskaya. Map p 131.*

Ice Palace PROSPECT BOLSHEVIKOV   When the international stars come to town, they come here: Bob Dylan, Pussycat Dolls, Iggy Pop et al. *Prospect Pyatiletok d. 1.* ☎ *812 718 6620,* ☎ *812 718 6622. Ticket prices vary. Metro: Prospect Bolshevikov. Map p 134.*

Oktyabrsky Concert Hall LIGOVSKY PROSPECT   A somewhat soulless venue, but retro-heaven for 1970s nostalgists. *Ligovsky Prospect d. 6.* ☎ *812 275 1300,* ☎ *812 275 1273 (answerphone). Ticket prices*

Extreme Sports

St Petersburg offers a surprising number of options for thrill-seekers. Tandem paragliding flights are available at the Uglovo airfield for a bargain 800R (☎ 812 298 3751, www.glide.ru), and tandem sky-dives at the Kasimovo aerodrome from 4,600R (☎ 8 921 865 6696, www.skydiving.ru). Alternatively, real extremists (or the outright bonkers) might like to try a parachute jump with the Sosnoborsky Aeroclub: a short distance from the nuclear power plant of the same name. Tandem jump with instructor 4,500R, Apr–Oct only. ☎ 8 813 692 5804. www.kummolovo.ru/eng/.

vary. Metro: Ploshad Vosstaniya. Map p 133.

Petrovsky Stadium PETROGRAD-SKAYA   The home ground of local team (and 2008 UEFA Cup winners) FC Zenit, at least until the new Kirov Stadium opens in 2010 (see p 106). Tickets are mainly sold through agencies: see website for details, or see Tickets p 137. *Petrovsky Island 2G. ☎ 812 328 8901, ☎ 812 328 8903. FC Zenit ticket department: ☎ 812 315 6202, ☎ 812 328 8902. www.petrovsky.spb.ru, www.fc-zenit.ru. Ticket prices vary. Metro: Sportivnaya. Map p 131.*

St Petersburg for Kids

Bowling City SENNAYA PLOSHAD A 24-hour, 36-lane complex with bars, VIP-halls, billiards, a shooting range, and 'home cinema' for the grown ups. *Sennaya Shopping Mall, Ul. Efimova d. 3. ☎ 812 380 3005. www.bowlingcity.ru. Tickets 360R–960R per hour. Metro: Sennaya Ploshad. Map p 132.*

Dolphinarium KRESTOVSKY OSTROV   Dolphins, white whales, and a performing seal. Plus the chance to swim with dolphins after the show. *Konstantinovsky Prospect d. 19. ☎ 812 235 4631, ☎ 812 380 9545. For information on swimming with dolphins call ☎ 812 961 3354.*

Tickets 200R–300R adults, 100R–200R kids. Metro: Krestovsky Ostrov. Map p 131.

Horrors of St. Petersburg ★★ PIONERSKAYA PLOSHAD   A good, highly interactive trip through the city's ghoulish underbelly: take the kids through the excellent English-language web pages before you go. *Planet Neptune Shopping Center, Ul. Marata d. 86. ☎ 812 313 0704, www.spbhorror.ru. Tickets 600R adults, 500R kids aged 12 and over. Metro: Pushkinskaya. Map p 132.*

Kart Center LENINSKY PROSPECT The first choice for boy racers. *Krasnoputilovskaya Ul. d. 69, 5th Floor. ☎ 812 703 1493, ☎ 812 703 1490. Tickets: from 320R for 5 min. Metro: Leninsky Prospect. Map p 134.*

Kart Land VASILIEVSKY OSTROV Another karting venue, rather closer to town. Hold your own 'mini-tournament' for groups of five or more. *Kozhevennaya Linya d. 1/3. ☎ 812 715 8441, ☎ 812 334 1211. Tickets 200R for 5 min, 300R for 10 min. Metro: Vasileostrovskaya, then marshrutki K359, K349, K273a. Map p 131.*

★★★ Oceanarium PIONERSKAYA PLOSHAD   Kids will doubtless head for the Shark Show (Tues–Sun, 7pm), but this very well designed

5,000 square meter complex fields more than 4,500 species, with displays including a Tropical Forest, Coral Reef, and habitats of the Russian North West. *Planet Neptune Shopping Center, Ul. Marata d. 86.* ☎ *812 448 0077. www.planeta-neptun.ru/eng/oceanarium/. Tickets 300R–500R adults, 150R–350R kids, 80R five to seven year-olds, under fives free. Metro: Pushkinskaya. Map p 132.*

The Great St Petersburg Circus FONTANKA

A city landmark, founded in 1877, this is highly rated for its clowns, acrobats, and 'Circus on Water' shows, although featuring a number of live animal acts, unfortunately. *Nab. Reki Fontanki d. 3.* ☎ *812 570 5390,* ☎ *812 570 5411. www.circus.spb.ru. Tickets 300R–1,000R. Metro: Gostiny Dvor. Map p 133.*

Swimming

kids Neptune Sport & Leisure Complex OBVODNOVO CANAL

Public pools may insist on a *spravka* (health certificate) before they will allow you to use a pool. If your hotel doesn't have a pool, come here for a 25-meter sport pool, children's pool with slides, jacuzzi, and sauna. *Lorum* ipsum. *Nab. Obvodnovo Kanala d. 93a.* ☎ *812 324 4610,* ☎ *812 324 4696. http://sport. neptun.spb.ru/eng/. Tickets 850R per hour. Metro: Pushkinskaya. Map p 132.*

★★★ kids Waterville PRIMOR-SKAYA

The perfect family day out, with six waterslides, a wave pool, pool with climbing wall, and an 'aquarium pool' with exotic fish behind glass. Be aware though that city authorities ordered it to close in April this year, after excessive chlorine use poisoned some swimmers. Trust your instincts if the water stings or the smell seems a bit strong. *Pribaltiskaya Hotel, Ul. Korablestroitelei d. 14.* ☎ *812 324 4700. www.waterville.ru. Tickets weekdays from 630R adults, 490R kids; weekends 790R adults, 570R kids. Metro: Primorskaya, then marshrutki 162, 148, 248, 162, 183, 7, 349. Map p 131.* ●

Lodging Best Bets

Best for **Aesthetes**
★★★ Alexander House Hotel
$$$$$ *Nab. Kryukovo Kanala d. 27*
(p 146)

Best for **Backpackers**
★★★ St Petersburg International
Hostel $ *3rd Sovetskaya d. 28 (p 154)*

Best for a **Bargain**
Holiday Inn Moskovskiye Vorota
$$$ *Moskovsky Prospect d. 97a*
(p 151)

Best for **Breakfast**
Renaissance St Petersburg Baltic
Hotel $$$$$ *Pochtamskaya Ulitsa*
d. 4 (p 153)

Best for **Breakfast in Bed**
★★★ Angleterre Hotel $$$$ *Malaya*
Morskaya Ulitsa d. 24 (p 146)

Best on a **Budget**
★★★ Idilliya Inn $$ *Ul. Marata d. 21*
(p 151)

Best for **Communist Kitsch**
Oktyabrskaya Hotel $$$ *Ligovsky*
Prospect d. 10 (p 152)

Best for **Families**
★★★ Novotel St Petersburg Center
$$$$$ *Ulitsa Mayakovskaya d. 3a*
(p 152)

Best for **Kids**
★★ Sokos Hotel Palace Bridge
$$$ *Birzhevoy Pereulok d. 2–4*
(p 153)

Best for **Lovers**
★★★ Grand Hotel Europe $$$$$
Mikhailovskaya Ulitsa d. 1/7
(p 150)

Best for a **Lovers' Tiff**
Royal Antares Hotel $$ *Nevsky*
Prospect d. 147 (p 153)

Best for **Pre-revolutionary
Glamour**
★★★ Taleon Imperial Hotel $$$$$
Nab. Reki Moiki d. 59 (p 154)

Best **Spa**
Sokos Hotel Palace Bridge
$$$ *Birzhevoy Pereulok d. 2–4*
(p 153)

Communist kitsch at Oktyabrskaya.

The Northern Islands **Lodging**

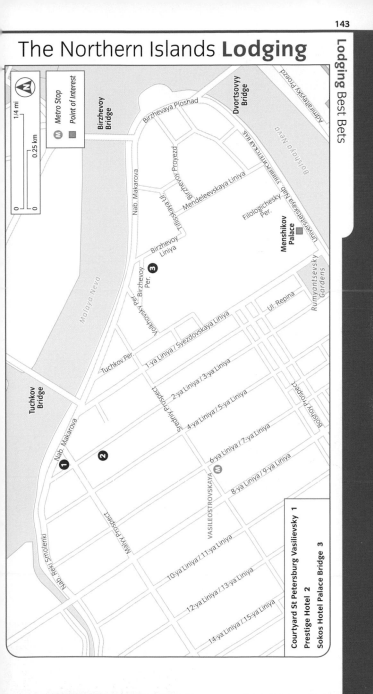

Courtyard St Petersburg Vasilievsky 1

Prestige Hotel 2

Sokos Hotel Palace Bridge 3

West of Nevsky **Lodging**

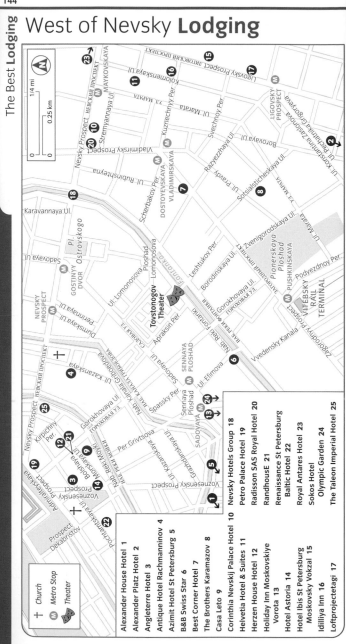

Alexander House Hotel **1**
Alexander Platz Hotel **2**
Angleterre Hotel **3**
Antique Hotel Rachmanninov **4**
Azimit Hotel St Petersburg **5**
B&B Swiss Star **6**
Best Corner Hotel **7**
The Brothers Karamazov **8**
Casa Leto **9**
Corinthia Nevskij Palace Hotel **10**
Helvetia Hotel & Suites **11**
Herzen House Hotel **12**
Holiday Inn Moskovskiye
  Vorota **13**
Hotel Astoria **14**
Hotel Ibis St Petersburg
  Moskovsky Vokzal **15**
Idililya Inn **16**
Loftprojectetagi **17**

Nevsky Hotels Group **18**
Petro Palace Hotel **19**
Radisson SAS Royal Hotel **20**
Randhouse **21**
Renaissance St Petersburg
  Baltic Hotel **22**
Royal Antares Hotel **23**
Sokos Hotel
  Olympic Garden **24**
The Taleon Imperial Hotel **25**

East of Nevsky **Lodging**

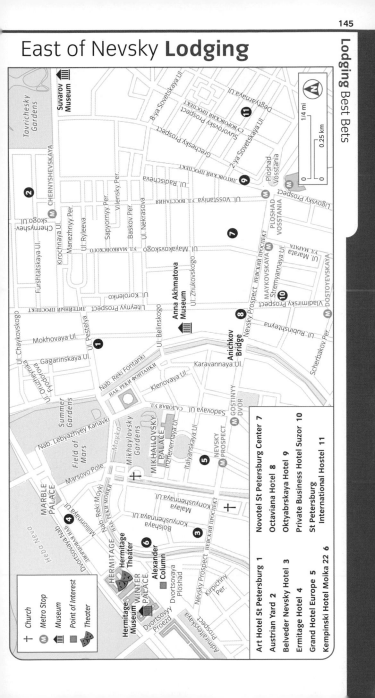

Legend
- + Church
- Ⓜ Metro Stop
- 血 Museum
- ■ Point of Interest
- ♦ Theater

Art Hotel St Petersburg 1

Austrian Yard 2

Belveder Nevsky Hotel 3

Ermitage Hotel 4

Grand Hotel Europe 5

Kempinski Hotel Moika 22 6

Novotel St Petersburg Center 7

Octaviana Hotel 8

Oktyabrskaya Hotel 9

Private Business Hotel Suzor 10

St Petersburg
International Hostel 11

St Petersburg **Lodging A to Z**

★★★ Alexander House Hotel

KOLOMNA   lWhile a second venue has now opened on Bolshaya Monetnaya, it was this hotel (a stone's throw from the Mariinsky) which really set the standard for boutique mini hotels when this mid-19th-century mansion was converted from former communalka apartments in 2003. Rooms are themed on international cities (Barcelona, Paris, etc.), and there's an on-site restaurant, elegant 1,500-book library, and high-speed Internet. *Nab. Kryukovo Kanala d. 27.* ☎ *812 575 3877. www.a-house.ru. 19 rooms. Doubles from 5,040R–8.640R w/breakfast (low season) to 8,280R–15,120R (high season). MC, V. Metro: Sadovaya, Sennaya Ploshad. Map p 144.*

Alexander Platz Hotel LIGOV-

SKY   Part of the Eurasia Hotels group, whose other venues include the Hotel Amsterdam and Hotel Regina. Given the facilities here—on-site restaurant and sauna with pool—the low season rates, in particular, are a bargain. Check the website for weekend discounts of up to 20%. *Vorozenskaya Ul. d 53.* ☎ *812 490 4810. www.eurasia-hotel.ru. 47 rooms. Doubles 2,150R–3,450R (low season) to 3,200R–4,000R (high season). MC, V. Metro: Ligovsky Prospect. Map p 144.*

★★★ Angleterre Hotel ST

ISAAC'S SQUARE   A perfect Art Deco interior, and one of the city's historic gems: poet Sergei Yesenin (husband of Isadora Duncan) committed suicide here in 1925. But this will always be my favorite hotel simply for its flawless attention to detail: breakfast in bed with rolls still hot from the oven, presented on a full service of Lomonosov Cobalt china. *M. Morskaya Ul. d. 24.* ☎ *812 494 5666. www.angleterrehotel. com/. 208 rooms. Standard doubles 8,750R–10,150R (low season) to 14,700R–16,800R (high season). AE, MC, DC, V. Metro: Nevsky Prospect, Gostiny Dvor. Map p 144.*

★★★ Antique Hotel Rachman-

ninov NEVSKY PROSPECT   The composer's residence from 1884–1885 (try and get the Lux Room, his

Angleterre Hotel.

Kitchenette, Austrian Yard apartment.

study), every room is furnished with antiques from the *Serebrianny Vek* (Silver Age). There's also an on-site photo gallery, Rachmanninov Dvorik, and WiFi in all rooms. *Kazanskaya Ul. d. 5.* ☎ *812 327 7466. http://hotelrachmaninov.com. 26 rooms. Doubles 4,350R–8,650R w/breakfast (low season) to 6,200R–13,300R (high season). DC, MC, V. Metro: Nevsky Prospect, Gostiny Dvor. Map p 144.*

Art Hotel St. Petersburg

LITEINY   A well-located mini hotel with bigger than average rooms,

A City of Mini Hotels

The city's tri-centennial in 2003 saw the opening of more than 500 mini hotels: which ought to make this a bargain location for tourists. The White Nights, however, can see the best-known venues (and many apartments) double their off-season rates. Don't stand for it. A bit of research can uncover a bargain, even in high summer. Start with the St Petersburg Small Hotels Association at www.innspb.com. Don't nurture any great expectations, however. The vast majority of the mini hotels are converted *communalki* (Soviet apartments with several families sharing a kitchen and bathroom). Most will offer Western standard bathrooms, a reasonable approximation of *evroremont* (Western refurbishment), scrupulous cleanliness, basic breakfasts and, these days, WiFi. But you do need to be prepared for scruffy entrances (often with well-concealed intercoms) and no elevators. Be careful when booking direct: some mini hotels may charge (in some instances quite steeply) for registering your visa, or for issuing a visa support letter. Unless you're here for less than three days (in which case you are not required to register at all), there's little you can do about this, particularly once you've arrived. But if negotiation fails, try securing a booking (and free invitation letter) through a tour agency.

New Openings

Going to press shortly after the stock market crash of October 2008, it's a moot point whether the recent spate of glitzy hotel openings will continue apace in the medium term. New openings scheduled before the crunch hit, however, include a second Sokos hotel on Vasilievsky Island, due to open in early 2009 (www.sokoshotels.fi), a **Starwood W** on Vosnesensky Prospect, due to open in June 2009 (www.starwood.com), and a **Four Seasons**, due to open in late 2009 in the former Lobanov-Rostovsky palace on Admiralteisky Prospect (www.fourseasons.com). InterContinental Hotels Group are due to open the 176-room **Staybridge Suites St Petersburg-Moskovskie Vorota** in spring 2009 (on the site of the recently refurbished Holiday Inn, see p 151).

breakfast in bed, and free high-speed Internet. Online bookings earn a 15% discount, with a further 5% discount for payment in cash. *Mokhovaya Ul. d. 27–29.* ☎ *812 740 7585. http://eng.art-hotel.ru. 14 rooms. Standard doubles from 4,025R. MC, V. Metro: Chernishevskaya. Map p 145.*

Austrian Yard LITEINY   Four individually crafted apartments complete with kitchenettes and all equipment. Plus on-site sauna and a free packed lunch. *Furshtatskaya Ul. d. 45.* ☎ *812 579 8235. www.austrianyard.com. 4 rooms. Doubles 3,776R–4,720R (low season) to 4,484R–5,428R (high season). MC, V. Metro: Chernishevskaya. Map p 145.*

Azimit Hotel St Petersburg

FONTANKA   Some distance from the main sights (although only a two-stop metro ride from Nevsky), recent refurbishment and a warren-like atmosphere don't quite disguise the 'Sovetskaya' hotel this once

Belveder Nevsky Hotel.

Corinthia Nevskij Palace Hotel.

was. But with 1,030 rooms and reasonable rates even in high season, it's a good standby for late bookers. *Lermontovsky Prospect d. 43/1.* ☎ *812 740 2640. http://eng.azimut hotels.ru. 1,030 rooms. Standard doubles 2,900R–3,200R w/breakfast (low season) to 4,900R–5,600R (high season). AE, MC, DC, V. Metro: Technologichesky Institute. Map p 144.*

B&B Swiss Star SENNAYA PLOSHAD Beautifully minimalist, with all the crisp efficiency you would expect. A help-yourself-anytime breakfast policy, free WiFi, and some interconnecting rooms for families: be aware though that not all rooms are en suite. *Nab. Reki Fontanki d. 93/26.* ☎ *8 911 929 2793. www.swiss-star.ru. 4 rooms. Doubles 2,100R–2,450R w/breakfast (low season) to 2,415R–3,815R (high season). MC, V. Metro: Sadovaya, Sennaya Ploshad. Map p 144.*

Belveder Nevsky Hotel NEVSKY PROSPECT Furnishings and décor are well above average here, and the location (in a small pedestrianized street just off Nevsky) perfect for light sleepers. Satellite TV, WiFi, minibar and, unusually, 24-hour room service. *B. Konushennaya d. 29.* ☎ *812 571 8338. http://hotel belveder-nevsky.com/01eng.html. 34 rooms. Doubles 3,150R–4,800R w/breakfast (low season) to 3,750R–5,700R (high season). DC, MC, V. Metro: Nevsky Prospect, Gostiny Dvor. Map p 145.*

Best Corner Hotel VLADIMIRSKAYA So called for its location at the center of the 'Five Corners' junction (and a stone's throw from Vladimirsky Prospect and Ulitsa Rubensteina, two of the city's best streets for shopping and dining), given the excellent level of refurbishment this is a very reasonably priced venue indeed. *Zagorodny Prospect d. 11.* ☎ *812 713 1392. www.bestcorner.spb.ru. 14 rooms. Standard doubles 4,440R–4,800R (low season) to 4,480R–5,980R (high season). MC, V. Metro: Dostoevskaya, Vladimirskaya. Map p 144.*

Casa Leto ST ISAAC'S SQUARE Fabulous location and larger than average rooms (all of them exquisitely furnished). Summer rates, however, are a bit too steep for what is, fundamentally, a mini hotel. *B. Morskaya d. 34.* ☎ *812 600 1096. www.casaleto.com. 5 rooms. Doubles 5,425R–7,350R w/breakfast (low season) to 7,525R–9,275R (high* *season). AE, MC, V. Metro: Nevsky Prospect, Gostiny Dvor. Map p 144.*

Corinthia Nevskij Palace Hotel

NEVSKY PROSPECT   Full service five star, again offering super-decadent (3,050R) Sunday brunches following refurbishment of its lobby and restaurant. Don't worry about proximity to Nevsky: all rooms are soundproofed. *Nevsky Prospect d. 57.* ☎ *812 380 2001. www.corinthia. ru. 281 rooms. Standard doubles from 9,000R (low season) to 25,165R (high season). MC, V. Metro: Mayakovskaya. Map p 144.*

Courtyard St Petersburg Vasilievsky

VASILIEVSKY OSTROV A new opening in October 2008, promising reasonably priced corporate-standard facilities—in low season at least. *2nd Line d. 61/30 VSO.* ☎ *812 380 4011. www.marriott. com. 218 rooms. Doubles from 5,900R (low season) to 13,500R (high season). MC, V. Metro: Vasileostrovskaya. Map p 143.*

Ermitage Hotel

DVORTSOVAYA NABEREZHNAYA   Surprisingly well priced, given its location minutes from the Hermitage. Modest but inoffensive furnishings (with a real fireplace and marble floor in the

Hotel Astoria.

hall), plus satellite TV and a free DVD library. *Millionnaya Ul. d. 11.* ☎ *812 571 5497. www.ermitagehotel.com. 4 rooms. Standard doubles 4,300R–8.600R (low season) w/ breakfast to 5.500R–11,000R (high season). MC, V. Metro: Nevsky Prospect, Gostiny Dvor. Map p 145.*

★★★ Grand Hotel Europe

NEVSKY PROSPECT   Pyotr Tchaikovsky's honeymoon hotel, and what must be the most romantic venue in town. Dripping luxury from its Art Deco entrance to its notoriously decadent Sunday brunches, this is the hotel of choice for anyone wanting to splurge: and those who can't will find very democratic attitudes to those sneaking in for drinks in the Lobby Bar or afternoon tea in the Mezzanine Café. Book carefully: it's astonishing what bargains a timely online reservation can turn up. *Mikhailovskaya Ul. d. 1/7.* ☎ *812 329 6000. www.grandhotel europe.com. 301 rooms. Standard doubles from 12,000R (low season) to 23,400R (high season). AE, DC, MC, V. Metro: Nevsky Prospect, Gostiny Dvor. Map p 145.*

Helvetia Hotel & Suites

VLADIMIRSKAYA   Consistently good service, larger than average rooms, and steps from Nevsky. Light sleepers might want to request rooms facing the courtyard. On-site Marius Pub (with restaurant) open 24 hours. *Ul. Marata d. 11.* ☎ *812 326 5353. http://en.helvetia-suites.ru. 75 rooms. Doubles 7,300R–8,700R w/ breakfast (low season) to 12,250R– 14,000R (high season). Suites (with kitchen) from 9,750R (low season) to 16,100R (high season). MC, V. Metro: Mayakovskaya. Map p 144.*

Herzen House Hotel

ST ISAAC'S SQUARE   Very central mini hotel with free WiFi, free tea and coffee, and no charges for visa support or registration. *B. Morskaya d. 25.*

☎ 812 315 5550. www.web.ru. 20 rooms. Doubles 3,100R–3,800R w/breakfast (low season) to 3,800R–5,200R (high season). AE, DC, MC, V. Metro: Nevsky Prospect, Gostiny Dvor. Map p 144.

Holiday Inn Moskovskiye Vorota MOSKOVSKY PROSPECT
Reopened in November 2008 after complete refurbishment, it now offers a fitness center with sauna and pool, satellite TV, and WiFi in all rooms, two bars and three restaurants (free for kids). *Moskovsky Prospect d. 97A.* ☎ 812 448 7171. *www.ichotelsgroup.com. 555 rooms. Doubles from 2,975R. Summer rates not yet published. AE, DC, MC, V. Metro: Moskovskiye Vorota. Map p 144.*

★★★ Hotel Astoria ST ISAAC'S SQUARE
Personally I prefer the next door Angleterre, but this is widely considered the better (or at least more luxurious) venue. Local legend has it that Hitler planned to hold his victory ball here, misguidedly anticipating victory in 1941. Rooms can be small and cramped, but the location is flawless and the facilities (including full-service spa with sauna and hamam) first class. *B. Morskaya d. 39.* ☎ 812 494 5757. *www.thehotelastoria.com. 213 rooms. Standard doubles from 12,000R (low season) to 22,260R (high season). AE, DC, MC, V. Metro: Nevsky Prospect, Gostiny Dvor. Map p 144.*

Hotel Ibis St Petersburg Moskovsky Vokzal LIGOVSKY
Opened in summer 2008, this is a welcome addition to the midrange sector. Short on frills, but with Western décor, plumbing, and facilities (including WiFi and air conditioning) guaranteed. *Ligovsky Prospect d. 54.* ☎ 812 622 0100. *www.ibishotel.com. 221 rooms. Doubles 3,750R (low season) to 6,500R (high season).*

AE, DC, MC, V. Metro: Ploshad Vosstaniya. Map p 144.

Idilliya Inn VLADIMIRSKAYA
It has its downside: the Soviet fixtures and fittings have not been entirely eradicated, and the breakfasts are gruesome. But it's very central, scrupulously clean, the bathrooms are modern, and it maintains competitive rates right through the summer. *Kuznechny Per. d. 18.* ☎ 812 713 1819. *www.idilliainn.ru. 21 rooms. Doubles from 1,600R w/ breakfast (low season) to 2,500R (high season). MC, V. Metro: Vladimirskaya, Dostoevskaya, Mayakovskaya. Map p 144.*

Kempinski Hotel Moika 22
ADMIRALTEISKAYA   Full-service five star, with some of the best on-site dining in town. Online promotions can secure substantial discounts. *Nab. Reki Moiki d. 22.* ☎ 812 335 9111. *www.kempinski-st-petersburg.com. 197 rooms. Doubles 8.140R–12,875R (low season) to 17,000R–24,800R (high season). AE, DC, MC, V. Metro: Gostiny Dvor. Map p 145.*

Loftprojectetagi LIGOVSKY PROSPECT
Super-hip hostel attached to the gallery of the same name. See p 94. *Ligovsky Prospect d. 74.* ☎ 812 441 3665, ☎ 782 2128. *http://lofthostel.ru. Dorms 600R. Metro: Ligovsky Prospect, Ploshad Vosstaniya. Map p 144.*

Nevsky Hotels Group NEVSKY PROSPECT
This group's six hotels run to the upper end of the mini hotels market, but they also offer private apartments, a hostel, and a new budget facility (Sky Hotel) opened in June 2008. Check the website for offers including 50% discounts on weekend rates and occasional 20% weekday reductions in low season. *Various addresses: see website for details.* ☎ 812 703 3860. *www.hon.ru. Doubles at the*

Novotel St Petersburg Center.

Sky Hotel start at 1,500R. MC, V. Metro: Nevsky Prospect, Gostiny Dvor. Map p 144.

★★★ **kids** **Novotel St Petersburg Center** NEVSKY PROSPECT Essentially a good four-star business hotel, but a good deal for families, with up to two children sleeping free in parents' rooms. *Ul. Mayakovskovo d. 3a.* ☎ *812 335 1188. www.accorhotels.com. 233 rooms. Doubles 7,600R–12,600R (low season) to 10,000R–14,000R (high season). MC, V. Metro: Mayakovskaya. Map p 145.*

Octaviana Hotel NEVSKY PROSPECT Somewhat spartan, but certainly functional and included by virtue of its non-ripoff year-round rates. *Nevsky Prospect d. 74–76.* ☎ *812 322 5076. www.octaviana. spb.ru. 17 rooms. Doubles 3,300R–3,600R w/breakfast (low season) to 3,800R–4,200R (high season). MC, V. Metro: Gostiny Dvor. Map p 145.*

Oktyabrskaya Hotel PLOSHAD VOSTANNIYA Probably one for nostalgists: both the main building and its 'filial' failing to disguise their former Soviet selves. Its history is pretty grim, too, having been used as a hospital for the starving during

the Siege of Leningrad, and the filial, as taxi drivers will no doubt tell you, until quite recently a *communalka* apartment building. *Ligovsky Prospect d. 10.* ☎ *812 717 7281. www. hoteloktiabrskaya.ru. 551 rooms (filial 111). Standard doubles 4,200R–5,000R and 2,900R–3,700R at the filial (low season) to 6,000R–6.900R and 4,200R–5,200R at the filial (high season). AE, DC, MC, V. Metro: Ploshad Vostanniya. Map p 145.*

Petro Palace Hotel ST ISAAC'S SQUARE Service can be patchy, but this very reasonable four star comes with all mod cons: high speed Internet, mini bar, air conditioning, in-room movies, sauna, jacuzzi and a very elegant pool. *M. Morskaya d. 14.* ☎ *812 571 3006. www.petropalacehotel.com. 193 rooms. 2,800R–5,000R (low season) to 11,000R–20,000R (high season). MC, V. Metro: Nevsky Prospect, Gostiny Dvor. Map p 144.*

Prestige Hotel VASILIEVSKY OSTROV Bargain business hotels. The VSO location has the better rooms, but there's a more central second venue on Gorokhovaya Ulitsa. Be careful though: they charge a whopping 1,225R for an invitation letter, and another 525R to register you with the immigration authorities. *3rd Line d. 52.* ☎ *812 312 0405. www.prestige-hotels.com. 10 rooms. Doubles 2,500R–4,200R w/breakfast (low season.) to 3,700R–4,900R (high season). AE, DC, MC, V. Metro: Vasileostrovskayar. Map p 143.*

Private Business Hotel Suzor

VLADIMIRSKAYA   Vladimirsky Prospect has, latterly, become a quite glitzy area, offering shops and restaurants probably a bit more upmarket than Nevsky itself. This hotel is a gem, with all the benefits of its location at a fraction of the chain hotels that dominate here. *Vladimirsky Prospect d. 10.* ☎ *812 713 2269. www.suzor.ru. 7 rooms. Doubles 2,800R w/breakfast (low season) to 4,000R (high season). MC, V. Metro: Dostoevskaya, Vladimirskaya. Map p 145.*

Radisson SAS Royal Hotel

NEVSKY PROSPECT   Full service five star with sauna, pool, fitness center, and free in-room WiFi. *Nevsky Prospect d. 49/2.* ☎ *812 322 5000. www.radissonsas.com. 164 rooms. Doubles 7,700R–9,625R (low season) to 17,000R–26,300R (high season). AE, DC, MC, V. Metro: Mayakovskaya. Map p 144.*

RandhousE CITYWIDE   Three mini hotels throughout the city: all of them clean, modern, and well equipped. Included for their highly commendable practice of applying a single tariff throughout the year. *B. Morskaya d. 25 apt. 17 (see website for other addresses).* ☎ *812 314 6333. Reservations:* ☎ *8 921 407 7002. www. randhouse.ru. 17 rooms. Standard doubles 2,275R–3,325R w/breakfast. Rubles only. Metro: Gostiny Dvor, Nevsky Prospect. Map p 144.*

Renaissance St Petersburg Baltic Hotel ST ISAAC'S SQUARE

Flawless location and amenities (and key cards that let you jump the Hermitage queue) but beware if booking direct: their internal exchange rate can be punitive. *Pochtmamskaya Ul. d. 4.* ☎ *812 380 4001. www.marriott.com. 102 rooms. Doubles 7,800R (low season) to 18,500R (high season). MC, V. Metro: Gostiny Dvor, Nevsky Prospect. Map p 144.*

Royal Antares Hotel PLOSHAD

ALEXANDRA NEVSKOVO   Others may disagree (and the very 1970s décor isn't to everyone's taste), but this is a personal favorite. Lux rooms come with a small sitting room attached (perfect after a romantic tiff) and breakfast staff willing to boil your eggs to the half-minute. *Nevsky Prospect d. 147.* ☎ *812 717 1835. www.antares-hotels.com. 9 rooms. Standard doubles 3,600R–3,900R w/breakfast (low season) to 3,960R–4,800R (high season). MC, V. Metro: Ploshad Alexandra Nevskovo. Map p 144.*

Sokos Hotel Olympic Garden

MOSKOVSKY PROSPECT   The first of two new openings from Finland's leading hotel chain in 2008. A reasonable mid-budget option, fully refurbished, with WiFi in all rooms. *Bataisky Per. d. 3a.* ☎ *812 335 2270. www.sokoshotels.fi. 348 rooms. Doubles from 5,796R (low season). Summer rates not yet published. MC, V. Metro: Technologichesky Institute. Map p 144.*

kids Sokos Hotel Palace Bridge

VASILIEVSKY OSTROV   Opened in summer 2008, this claims to be Russia's first spa hotel. Families will appreciate the child-friendly rooms (and promising 26 time-share apartments), but the real draw here is the saunas—no fewer than eight, including a traditional Turkish hamam, a snow sauna (with real snow), and the somewhat disturbing sauna cave. Plus, of course, a jacuzzi, plunge pool, and tropical shower. *Birzhevoi Per.*

The Taleon Imperial Hotel.

d. 2–4, VSO. ☎ 812 335 2200. www.
holidayclubspa.com. 285 rooms.
Standard doubles from 8,000R (low
season). AE, DC, MC, V. Metro: Vasileostrovskaya. Map p 143.

St Petersburg International
Hostel PLOSHAD VOSTANNIYA
The first of the now ubiquitous hostels: basic but scrupulously clean. A
frequent standby for those in extre-
mis and on a budget. *3rd Sovetskaya d. 28.* ☎ 812 329 8018. www.
ryh.ru. Dorm beds from 600R, doubles from 800R. MC, V. Metro: Ploshad Vosstaniya. Map p 145.

The Brothers Karamazov
VLADIMIRSKAYA   So called for its
proximity to the Dostoevsky apartment museum (and with rooms
named to match his most famous
heroines), this is a well-priced,
well-equipped mini hotel with air
conditioning and WiFi throughout.
Sotsialisticheskaya Ul. d. 11a.
☎ 812 335 1185. http://karamazov
hotel.com. 28 rooms. Standard
doubles 3,700R (low season)

w/breakfast to 5,500R (high season).
MC, V. Metro: Dostoevskaya, Vladimirskaya. Map p 144.

★★★ The Taleon Imperial
Hotel NEVSKY PROSPECT   Better
known for its top-tier dining (see
p 117) the restored Yeliseev mansion also offers 29 uniquely decorated suites and rooms. Its sheer
opulence would suggest it's beyond
the reach of all but the oligarchs,
but you might be surprised. While
suites can cost up to 213,750 rubles
per night, you can find low season
promotional offers for as little as
10,500R. For a study in real New
Russian luxury, however, take a look
at the website of its affiliate Taleon
Residence: the former Sheremetyev
Palace, flawlessly restored and available for a mere 868,000 rubles per
night. *Nab. Reki Moiki d. 59.* ☎ 812
324 9911. www.eliseevpalacehotel.
com. 29 rooms. Standard doubles
from 10,500R (low season) and up.
AE, DC, MC, V. Metro: Nevsky Prospect, Gostiny Dvor. Map p 144. ●

10 The Best Day Trips & Excursions

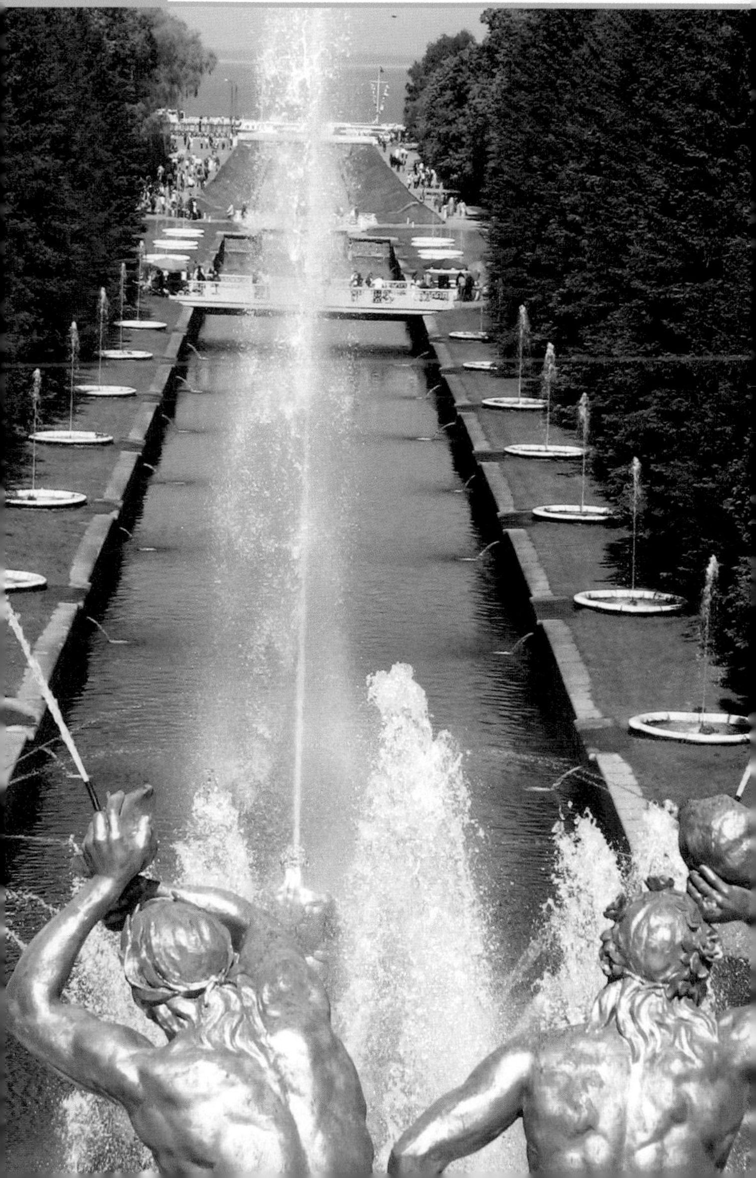

Tsarskoye Tselo

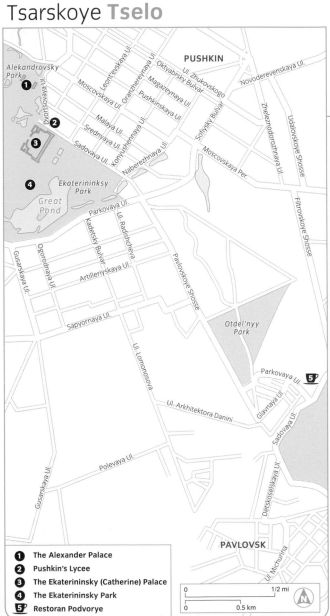

1 The Alexander Palace
2 Pushkin's Lycee
3 The Ekaterininsky (Catherine) Palace
4 The Ekaterininsky Park
5 Restoran Podvorye

Decadent' doesn't even begin to do it justice: the Baroque excess of Tsarskoye Tselo's Grand Palace makes today's oligarchs look like paragons of thrift. Painstakingly restored after obliteration by the Nazis in WWII, it's worth the hour-long trip from the center for the Amber Room alone. This tour covers the 'must see' sights only, allowing time for a quick tour of the equally elaborate grounds. START: **With Pushkin's Lycee and the Alexander Palace, both passed en route.**

❶ The Alexander Palace. The austere Classicism of the Alexander Palace, built in 1792–1800 by Giacomo Quarenghi for Catherine II's grandson, the future Alexander I, stands in stark contrast to the Baroque excess of the Ekaterininsky. Later used as the summer residence of Tsar Nicholas II, the Imperial family was kept under house arrest here from March–July 1917. The palace was used as a hospital for German SS officers during WWII, with the dead allegedly buried in the grounds. A permanent exhibition now records the palace as it was under Nicholas II. *Sadovaya*

Ul. d. 7. Admission 300R adults, 150R concessions. Daily 10am–5pm. Closed Tues and last Wed of every month.

❷ Pushkin's Lycee. Originally part of the Catherine Palace (intended to keep the royal children out of sight), this building was closed for refurbishment in December 2008. Its famous alumni, somewhat ironically, include several members of the Decembrist uprising, in addition to Alexander Pushkin, a student here from 1811–1817. *Sadovaya Ul. d.12. Daily 10.30am–4.30pm. Closed Tues.*

The Amber Room

Originally constructed in 1701–1709 within the Charlottesburg Palace, the panels of what was to become Tsarskoye Tselo's Amber Room were given by the Prussian king Friedrich Wilhelm I to his then ally Peter I in 1716. They were not unpacked and installed until 1755, however: a task which required some eight tons of amber and which took 10 years to complete. Attempts to protect it from the German invasion of 1941 proved futile: the panels were too fragile to move, and its disguise under wallpaper was discovered by the Nazis in less than 36 hours. Initially transferred to Konigsburg (now Kaliningrad), the original panels have never been recovered, and rumors of their current location abound. Some claim they were destroyed in the Allied bombing of Konigsburg, others that they were torpedoed in transit. A group of German treasure hunters claimed to have found evidence of them near the Czech border in early 2008. Reconstruction of the new Amber Room began in 1979 (with financial support from Germany), and it opened in 2003.

The Best Day Trips & Excursions

Tsarskoye Tselo: Getting There

Visiting Tsarskoye Tselo's palaces and parks might be expensive, but getting there needn't be. Take an *elektrichka* (suburban electric train) from Vitebsky Vokzal to Detskoe Selo (Pushkin), and then bus 371 or 382. Alternatively, take any of the myriad *marshrutki* (Nos K342, K286, K287, K545, K347) parked in front of the Dom Sovetov on Moskovsky Prospect (Moskovskaya metro). Expect to pay about 25R. The *marshrutki* will drop you at the end of Peterburgskoye Shosse, from where it's a half-mile walk down Dvortsovaya Ulitsa.

❸ ★★★ The Ekaterininsky (Catherine) Palace. Originally a small stone palace (built in 1717–1723) by Peter I's wife Empress Catherine I, it was Peter's daughter Empress Elizabeth who instructed Bartolomeo Rastrelli to redesign it (1752–1756) into what was to become one of the country's finest examples of Russian Baroque architecture. Catherine the Great, while deploring much of Elizabeth's excess, extended the palace and added many outbuildings in the Ekaterininsky Park (see p 159). Protocol is maddening: tourists are only allowed in between 12pm–2pm and 4pm–5pm in summer, and, visitors at any time of year must follow a fixed tour, herded into groups and held in an annexe until the curators deign to let you through. The tour does at least cover the main sights, including the Parade Staircase, the Great Hall (a 1,200 square meter extravaganza complete with ceiling painting), and the Amber Room. *Sadovaya Ul. d. 7. ☎ 812 465 2024 (Russian only), ☎ 812 465 9424 (administration). www.tzar.ru. Admission 550R adults, 280R concessions. Daily 10am–5pm. Closed Tues and last Mon of every month.*

Tsarskoye Tselo.

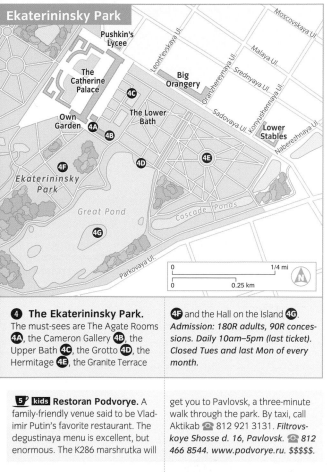

Ekaterininsky Park

Pushkin's Lycee

The Catherine Palace

Own Garden

Ekaterininsky Park

Great Pond

Big Orangery

The Lower Bath

Lower Stables

Cascade Ponds

4 4A 4B 4C 4D 4E 4F 4G

0 | 1/4 mi
0 | 0.25 km

4 The Ekaterininsky Park. The must-sees are The Agate Rooms 4A, the Cameron Gallery 4B, the Upper Bath 4C, the Grotto 4D, the Hermitage 4E, the Granite Terrace 4F and the Hall on the Island 4G. *Admission: 180R adults, 90R concessions. Daily 10am–5pm (last ticket). Closed Tues and last Mon of every month.*

5 kids Restoran Podvorye. A family-friendly venue said to be Vladimir Putin's favorite restaurant. The degustinaya menu is excellent, but enormous. The K286 marshrutka will get you to Pavlovsk, a three-minute walk through the park. By taxi, call Aktikab ☎ 812 921 3131. *Filtrovskoye Shosse d. 16, Pavlovsk. ☎ 812 466 8544. www.podvorye.ru. $$$$$.*

Staying Over

The Ekaterininsky Palace and parks will take you at least a day, and you may well want to explore the picturesque streets of Pushkin town itself, the Great Palace of neighboring Pavlovsk (see www.virtualpushkin.com). A good choice hotel is the Hotel Ekaterina, with doubles at 3,500R. *Hotel Ekaterina, Sadovaya Ul. d. 5a. ☎ 812 466 8042. www.hotelekaterina.ru.* In Pushkin, the Hotel Natalya has doubles from 2,900R. *Malaya Ul. d. 56a. ☎ 812 466 0277. www.hotelnatali.ru.*

Peterdvorets (Peterhof)

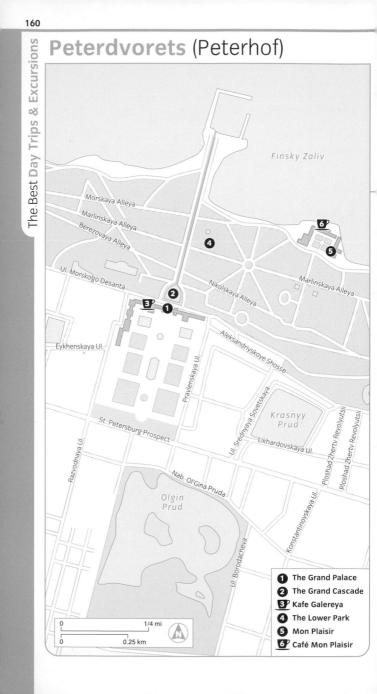

Finsky Zaliv

Morskaya Alleya

Marlinskaya Alleya

Berezovaya Alleya

Ul. Morskogo Desanta

④

Nikolskaya Alleya

Marlinskaya Alleya

⑥

⑤

Eykhenskaya Ul.

②
③ ①

Aleksandriyskoye Shosse

Pravlenskaya Ul.

St. Petersburg Prospect

Ul. Srednyaya Sovetskaya

Likhardovskaya Ul.

Krasnyy Prud

Ploshad Zhertv Revolyutsii

Ploshad Zhertv Revolyutsii

Razvodnaya Ul.

Nab. Ol'Gina Pruda

Konstantinovskaya Ul.

Olgin Prud

Ul. Borodacheva

| 0 | 1/4 mi |
| 0 | 0.25 km |

① The Grand Palace
② The Grand Cascade
③ Kafe Galereya
④ The Lower Park
⑤ Mon Plaisir
⑥ Café Mon Plaisir

Left in ruins after Nazi occupation in 1941–1943, it has taken almost 60 years to restore Peter the Great's 1709 gardens to their former glory. The result is stunning, but this is one location where the higher-prices-for-foreigners policy really starts to sting: visiting each of Peterhof's museums would cost more than 4,000R— or $160. Don't bother. The Grand Palace has some interesting exhibits and the Marly Palace holds personal possessions of Peter the Great, but otherwise, do what the locals do: take a packed lunch and spend the day getting drenched under the trick fountains of the Lower Park. **START: At the Grand Palace, looking out to the Gulf of Finland over the gilt statues of the Grand Cascade.**

❶ The Grand Palace. The version you see bears little resemblance to the 1721 original completed by Jean-Baptiste Le Blond, having been considerably extended by Francesco Bartolomeo Rastrelli on the instruction of Peter I's daughter Empress Elizabeth. Highlights include the Chesme Hall, hung with tapestries celebrating victory over the Turks in 1770, the Throne Hall, and the Chinese Study. *Razvodnaya Ul. d. 2.* ☎ *812 450 6527. Admission 520R adults, 250R concessions. Daily 10.30am–6pm (11am–6pm Oct–Apr), but note individual foreign tourists are admitted between 12pm–2pm and 4.15pm– 5pm only. Closed Mon and last Tues of every month.*

The Grand Palace.

❷ ★★★ The Grand Cascade. The centerpiece of the Main Cascade is the statue of Samson opening the jaws of a lion. Designed by Rastrelli and unveiled in 1735, it was commissioned to celebrate Peter's victory over the Swedes at Poltava in 1709. The version you see dates from 1947, the original having been looted by the Nazis. The grottoes underneath hide the Museum of Fountains: the entire complex is driven by gravity, with not a single pump used. Resist the impulse to head straight down the steps: bear eastwards downhill towards the Chess Cascade, best viewed from beneath.

❸ ★★★ Kafe Galereya. An elegant little café in the Western Gallery of the Grand Palace, offering cheap coffee and traditional Russian snacks. ☎ *812 450 7068. $.*

❹ ★★★ The Lower Park. Choosing when to visit can be tricky: the Grand Palace is closed on Tuesdays, Mon Plaisir and the Marly Palace are closed on Wednesdays, and are jam-packed at weekends. From mid-May to October though, the fountains never close. From the Chess Cascade it's a short walk north to Mon Plaisir, towards the Peter I statue and past two trick

The Grand Cascade.

fountains on either side: don't step on the pebbles near the Tree Fountain, and don't sit on the chairs beneath the Umbrella. Bring mosquito repellent if you expect to stay late. *Admission 300R adults, 150R concessions. Daily 9am–7pm, ticket office to 4.30pm. The fountains operate mid-May to mid-Oct, 11am–5pm (6pm Sat–Sun).*

5 Mon Plaisir. The first of the palaces to be built at Peterhof (and Peter I's favorite), save yourself 300 rubles and just press your nose against the floor-to-ceiling paned glass. ☎ *812 450 6129. Admission 300R adults, 150R concessions. Daily 10.30am–6pm. Closed Wed. and closed completely Oct–May. Peterhof, Razvodnaya Ul. d. 2. Excursions* ☎ *812 420 0073, information line (May–Oct)* ☎ *812 450 5287. http://peterhofmuseum.ru.*

6 Café Mon Plaisir. By far the best of the summer cafes. Cold beer or hot coffee looking out over the Gulf of Finland. ☎ *812 450 6106,* ☎ *812 450 6758. $.* ●

Peterhof: Getting There

Definitely a trip to make under your own steam. Excursions may look cheap, but they'll leave you steaming in Nevsky traffic in high season. Take the metro to the outskirts and pick up the K424 or K300 *marshrutki* from Avtovo metro or the K224 from Leninsky Prospect. Alternatively, it's a 45-minute train ride from Baltiysky Vokzal to Novy Peterhof, followed by a five-stop journey on buses 350, 351, 352, or 356. Best of all, head down to the Hermitage pier (directly in front of the Winter Palace) for a 30-minute, 350R trip by hydrofoil (or speedboat), or take a 15-minute helicopter flight (1,500R) from the Peter Paul Fortress (☎ 812 704 1676, ☎ 812 571 0084). Don't leave it too late heading home: queues for the marshrutki can be horrendous, and tour groups are given priority on hydrofoils. If you do get stuck, expect to pay 60R–100R for a taxi back to the station, or 800R–1,000R back to Nevsky Prospect. For taxis call: ☎ 812 428 6565, ☎ 812 421 0000, ☎ 812 727 6565.

The
Savvy Traveler

Before **You Go**

Government Tourist Offices

The Federal Agency for Tourism currently has no official representation abroad.

The Best Times to Go

The White Nights of June and July are unmissable, but you'll find long days, warm weather, and significantly lower hotel bills if you go in April or May. The sunny, wind-free days of *Babie Leto* (woman's summer) in September and October are perfect for walking the parks and canals. Christmas and New Year are best for parties and walks across the frozen Neva.

Visas & Registration

All visitors to Russia require a visa: there are no exceptions, and visas cannot be issued at the border. To apply for a visa you will need to submit:

- A valid 10-year passport, with at least one blank visa page (and some consulates may insist your passport be valid for six months after you travel).

- One passport photo.

- One completed visa application form.

- An invitation from an approved agency. If applying for a tourist visa this will be your tour agency or hotel, but note that accommodation must be reserved for the entire duration of the visa. You will be given an immigration card (in Russian and English) to complete on landing, and you will need to register your visa within three days of arriving in Russia: if you are traveling on a tourist visa, your hotel or inviting agency will do this for you. The following companies offer visa support

services including invitation procurement, and registration:

Real Russia Limited, 3 The Ivories, Northampton Street, Islington, London N1 2HY, UK (☎ 020 7100 7370. www.realrussia.co.uk). Their partner organization in the United States is Russia-Visa.com, Embassy Row, 2005 Massachusetts Avenue, Washington DC 20036 (☎ 1 800 567 4175 (tollfree), ☎ 1 202 250 3608). Russian National Group, 224 West 30th Street, Suite 701, New York, NY, 10001, USA (☎ 877 221 7120, ☎ 646 473 2233; www.russia-travel.com). www.RussianVisa.net maintains a list of companies offering Russian visa services worldwide. If you want to do it yourself, Russian consulates abroad include: Australia: 78 Canberra Avenue, Griffith, ACT 2603, ☎ +61 6 6295 9474, or 7–9 Fullerton Street Woollahra, Sydney, NSW 2025 (☎ 02 9326 1866, visa section direct line ☎ 02 9326 1188; www.sydney russianconsulate.com). Canada: 175 Bloor Street East, South Tower, Suite 801, Toronto, Ontario, M4W 3R8 (☎ 1 416 962 9911; www. toronto.mid.ru). Ireland: 184–186 Orwell Road, Rathgar, Dublin 14 (☎ 353 1 492 34 92; www.ireland. mid.ru). New Zealand: 57 Messines Road, Karori, Wellington (☎ 64 4 476 6113, consular department ☎ 64 4 476 6742; http://wellington. rusembassy.org). UK: Russian Embassy Consular Section, 5 Kensington Palace Gardens, London W8 4QS (☎ 020 3051 1199; ☎ 0845 868 1199; www.rusemblon.org). United States: 2650 Wisconsin Avenue, NW, Washington DC, 20007 (☎ 1 202 298 5700; www.russian-embassy.org). In New York: 9 East 91 Street, New York, NY, 10128 (☎ 1 212 348 0926).

- You may need to provide evidence of travel or medical insurance, but this varies, depending on what visa you apply for, and at what consulate.

Festivals & Special Events

SPRING. Maslenitsa (Mardi Gras) kicks off a week of blini-eating at stalls throughout town in honor of the Orthodox pre-Lent celebrations. **Defenders of the Motherland Day** (February 24th) is an opportunity for old army buddies to meet up and relive their national service, but **International Women's Day**, March 8th, is a serious day for the women in your life. **Victory Day**, May 9th, is one of the few old Soviet holidays still observed, with fireworks, parades, and proud veterans in the park.

SUMMER. It would be impossible to list all the festivals, free concerts, raves, and events that Petersburgers cram into their short summer. The **St Petersburg International Economic Forum** sees everyone come to out to ogle the oligarchs' yachts moored along the Neva, watch fireworks and laser shows from the Strelka (Spit) on Vasilievsky Island, or attend the (free) closing concert. A citywide festival for graduating high school students, **Aliye Parusa** (Red Sails) starts with tall ships floating down the Neva and ends (after fireworks, light shows, open-air concerts, and gas flares from the top of the Rostral Columns (see p 80) with every school leaver drinking their own weight in beer.

FALL. October sees Fashionistas gathering for **St Petersburg Fashion Week**, and tennis fans for the **St Petersburg Open**.

WINTER. The single biggest event of the year is **New Year's Eve**, when young revelers swarm the city to drink sweet champagne into the early hours. Now recognized with a public holiday, the **Orthodox Christmas** sees most of the population taking up to 10 days off work: leaving tourists free to wander unimpeded by traffic or crowds in the Hermitage.

The Weather
This is a wet and windy city, and if you're here at any time from October to May you'll need a fleece, an umbrella, and gloves. But breezes keep the city cool right through summer, with temperatures rarely exceeding 25 °C. January temperatures can average –10 °C, but cold snaps also mean crisp sunny days and spectacular sunsets over the Neva.

Cellphones
World phones—GSM phones—work in Russia, but roaming charges are extortionate. If your phone is not locked, it may be worth buying a St Petersburg SIM card. Some operators (Beeline (www.beeline.ru) and MegaFon (http://eng.megafon.ru)) may require evidence of registration in St Petersburg, but MTS cards (www.mtsgsm.com) can be purchased for about 150 rubles on production of your passport, with international calls on pay-as-you-go tariffs. Alternatively, buy an international calling card: Mango is one of the most reliable (and quite user-friendly for non-Russian speakers), available at most kiosks.

Car Rentals
Erratic drivers, poor quality roads, hopelessly inadequate parking space and corrupt traffic police make driving a challenge even for long-term residents. If you're determined to hire though, the following all have representation at Pulkovo airport and downtown:

Useful Websites

www.visit-petersburg.com: the St Petersburg Tourist Office site.
www.hermitagemuseum.org: the ticket queues are horrendous.
Book your ticket as soon as you've booked your flight.
www.sptimes.ru: the city's only English-language newspaper.
www.enlight.ru: Peter Sobolev's 'Wandering Camera' site, covering
the main streets, sights, and architecture.
www.expat.ru: well-established site maintained by long-standing
residents, includes a St Petersburg page.
www.redtape.ru: a recent competitor to www.expat.ru, again with
a page on St Petersburg.
www.waytorussia.net: its information is patchy and its nightlife list-
ings often outdated, but the Talk Lounge forum can be useful for
resolving visa, customs, and other sticky issues.

AVIS Rent a Car: offices at Pulkovo-1 and 2, and at the Moskva Hotel, Pl. Alexandra Nevskovo d. 2. ☎ 812 600 1213. www.avis-rentacar.ru. Europcar: offices at Pulkovo-2 (☎ +7 (8) 911 987 2956) and at Nevsky Prospect d. 29. ☎ 812 600 5145. www.europcar.ru. Hertz: offices at Pulkovo-1 and 2 and city locations including M. Morskaya Ul. d. 23. ☎ 812 326 4505. www.hertz. ru. Sixt: offices at Moskovsky Vokzal (☎ 812 493 4665, ☎ 812 309 0355 Sat–Sun) and Pulkovo-2 (☎ +7 (8) 952 236 9128 Mon–Fri, ☎ 812 309 0455 Sat–Sun. www.sixt.ru.

Getting **There**

By Plane

Getting into the city from Pulkovo-2 (the city's international terminal) involves a 20-minute bus ride to Moskovskaya metro (No. 13): tickets cost 16R and buses run every 5–15 minutes from 5.30am (6am Sat–Sun) to 0.45am. The Airport Express bus also runs round the clock between Pulkovo-1, Pulkovo-2, and Pushkinskaya metro. ☎ 812 388 0055 www. airportexpress.ru. Alternatively, the K3 and K213 *marshrutkas*—licensed mini cabs following fixed bus routes—will take you to Sennaya Ploshad in the center. You'll save money if you can arrange for a taxi to meet you on arrival: Taxi Sem Million (☎ 812 700 0000) charges 800R to the center, plus 4R per minute waiting time. If you haven't booked a taxi in advance, ignore the touts and head for the Baltcar desk, directly opposite as you come out of arrivals: expect to pay around 1,800R to Nevsky Prospect. Baltcar ☎ 812 707 5707. Find more information at www.pulkovoairport.ru. Pulkovo-1 ☎ 812 704 3822, Pulkovo-2 ☎ 812 704 3444. Direct flights to Moscow are inexpensive and bookable online through S7 Airlines (www.s7.ru) and Rossiya Russian Airlines (www.pulkovo.ru) or at the Central Ticket Agency, Nevsky Prospect d. 7/9 ☎ 812 315 0072 www.cavs.ru. Pulkovo Express will also deliver tickets to your hotel door: www.pulkovo-express.ru. Aeroflot also fly direct from Sheremetyevo (Moscow) to Domodedovo (St Petersburg) although transfers can be tiresome.

By Train

Trains from Eastern Europe, the Baltics, and Germany arrive at the beautiful Style Moderne Vitebsky Vokzal (see p 59, **5**) (Zagorodny Prospect d. 52 ☎ 812 768 5807), and those from Finland at Finlyandsky (Ploshad Lenina d. 6 ☎ 812 768 7687. Trains for Moscow leave from Moskovsky Vokzal (Ploshad Vosstaniya d. 2 ☎ 812 768 4597). All of these stations connect directly with the metro. For general rail enquiries (in Russian only) dial ☎ 812 768 7900. Avoid queues at stations and buy tickets in advance at the Central Train Ticket Office, Nab. Kanala Griboedova d. 24 ☎ 812 762 3344. A multi-lingual journey planner for European rail travel can be found on the German rail website www.bahn. de. Russian Railways maintain a site in English and Russian at www.rzd. ru, but you'll find more user-friendly information (including timetables in English) at www.trainsrussia.com.

By Coach

Eurolines have an office at Nab. Obvodnovo Kanala d. 118 (the Admiral Business Center) ☎ 812 441 3757. www.eurolines.ru. The City Bus Station offers routes to Helsinki and the Baltic countries (Nab. Obvodnovo Kanala d. 36 ☎ 812 766 5777) but the best bargains are to be found on Ploshad Vosstaniya, where coaches converge from late afternoon with departures to Helsinki, Riga, and Tallin and from as little as 500R: all of which offer cheap connections via easyJet.

Getting **Around**

By Metro

While it can't match Moscow's splendor (apart from a select few stations on Line 1), this is by far the cheapest and easiest way to see the city. Individual stations vary, but most are open from around 5.30am to 00.30am. *Zhetons* are 17 rubles each, available from the kassa or machines on the walls. Monthly bus/metro/tram and trolleybus tickets cost 1,000R, available from metro stations. Tickets for buses, trams, and trolleys only are available from kiosks throughout the city (with one just outside Ploshad Vostanniya metro) for 535R per month.

By Marshrutka

The central sights are all reasonably accessible, but beyond Nevsky Prospect and Palace Square you'll often be faced with a long walk from the metro. Thankfully, there are *marshrutki*—licensed mini-buses that follow fixed routes for a flat fare of around 25 rubles. Key stops are listed on their windows, but most will usually pick you up if you flag them down.

By Taxi

Any driver can legally pick up a passenger who flags him down. There are very few other cities in the world where this could be recommended, but in 15 years I have never encountered any problems. Have your destination written down in Russian, and start negotiating at 200 rubles for trips within the Fontanka: expect to pay double that for trips into Petrogradskaya, Vasilievsky Ostrov, or anywhere beyond the Obvodnoy Canal. Tips are not expected.

By Bus

It's possible to buy tickets for buses, trams, and trolleybuses onboard (about 22 rubles), but if you're here for some time you'll get fewer hostile stares if you buy cards in advance. A tourist city bus operates in summer, leaving Nevsky Prospect at the junction with Dumskaya Ulitsa and touring St Isaac's Cathedral, the Winter Palace, the Church of the Spilled Blood, and the Peter Paul Fortress. 500R adults, 350R kids, audio guide included. ☎ 812 710 5529.

By Car

It's improving, but with most road signs still in Cyrillic, driving is only viable for the experienced or the fluent.

On Foot

Sidewalks are dreadful: pack sturdy boots, even for non-winter trips. Well booted, there's no better way to see the city, but familiarize yourself with the key *marshrutka* and bus routes. Dom Knigi sells a very useful *City Transport Pocket Atlas* (Карманный Атлас Санкт-Петербург Городской Транспорт), in Russian, but with the main routes clearly shown.

Fast **Facts**

APARTMENT RENTALS Apartment rentals—particularly during the White Nights—aren't really that much of a bargain (particularly compared to rates at mini hotels), and quality can be highly variable. Insist on seeing photos by e-mail before you book. Among the most reliable is Pulford at Nab. Reki Moiki d. 6. ☎ 812 325 6277 www.pulford.ru. The waytorussia.net website offers an accommodation-finding service (including apartments, B&Bs, and hostels) but responses can be painfully slow. Windows on Nevsky, specializing in centrally located short-term rentals, can be a good bet for first-timers (www.w-o-n.ru).

ATMS/CASHPOINTS Be very, very careful when using cashpoints here. My first night researching this book was spent blocking cards after two cards were swallowed at two different ATMs, with 'emergency' numbers out of date. Stick to Raffaissen Bank or Citibank, both of which have branches on central Nevsky Prospect. It is now illegal to pay for goods and services in Russia in any currency other than rubles.

B&BS See Mini hotels, p 170. A stay with a local family can give a unique insight into the city as it is lived by most: the Host Families' Association (HOFA) has been placing guests with St Petersburg families since 1990. ☎ (8) 901 305 8874; ☎ 812 275 1992. www.hofa.ru.

BUSINESS HOURS Most banks open Mon–Fri 9am–8pm, Sat 9am–5pm. Citibank branches are open 10am–8pm daily, with many open Saturdays until 6pm. Museums typically open 10am–6pm with the last ticket sold up to an hour before closing, and restaurants open 12pm–12am (or last guest). Many supermarkets now open round the clock (including Lend, Vladimirsky Prospect d.19, and the larger branches of Perekroistok): and those that don't are usually open until 10pm.

CONSULATES AND EMBASSIES All of the following have consulates in St Petersburg:

AUSTRALIAN EMBASSY 11 Italianskaya Ul. d. 1. ☎ 812 325 1100. www.russia.embassy.gov.au.

BRITISH CONSULATE GENERAL Ploshad Proletarskoi Diktaturi d. 5. ☎ 812 320 3200. http://ukinrussia.fco.gov. uk/en.

CONSULATE GENERAL OF THE UNITED STATES Furshtatskaya Ul. d. 15. ☎ 812 331 2600. http://st petersburg.usconsulate.gov/.

CREDIT CARDS MasterCard and Visa are widely accepted, American Express less so and Diners Club hardly at all. Report lost credit cards on ☎ 812 718 6858 (Diners Club, Visa, Mastercard) and ☎ 812 326 4500, ☎ 812 329 6070 (AmEx www.americanexpress.com/russia/).

CUSTOMS See p 99 for restrictions on antiques and other items. You may bring in up to $3,000 worth of hard currency (including travelers checks) without declaring it, but sums above this should be declared on entry (and all amounts above $10,000 must be) to avoid problems when leaving. Travelers may take up to $10,000 out of the country, but note that this figure is inclusive of all hard currencies, rubles, and travelers checks.

DOCTORS See 'Emergencies'. The following provide Western-standard private medical care:

American Medical Clinic, Nab. Reki Molkl d. 78. ☎ 812 740 2090. www.amclinic.ru. **Euromed**, Suvorovsky Pr. d. 60. ☎ 812 327 0301. www.euromed.ru. **MEDEM International Clinic**, Ul. Marata d. 6. ☎ 812 336 3333. www.medem.ru. **Russian-Finnish Clinic Scandinavia**, Liteiny Prospect d. 55a. ☎ 812 336 7777. www.avaclinic.ru.

ELECTRICITY 220V AC, European two-pin plugs are standard.

EMERGENCIES Dial ☎ 01 for fire, ☎ 02 for police (or the hotline for foreigners on ☎ 812 578 3094), ☎ 03 for an ambulance and ☎ 04 if you smell gas.

GAY & LESBIAN TRAVELERS Decriminalized in 1993, Russia's gay community is discreet but active. Discovergaypetersburg.com is a full-service gay travel and tour company, with a very informative site. Gay.ru (http://english.gay.ru) has a short English language guide to St Petersburg, listing the main cafes, clubs, discos, and saunas.

HOLIDAYS New Year: January 1st. Note that January 2nd, 3rd, 4th and 5th are also public holidays, and offices close for up to a week. Orthodox Christmas: January 7th. Defenders of the Fatherland Day: February 23rd. International Women's Day: March 8th. Day of Spring and Labor: May 1st. Victory Day: May 9th. Russia Day: June 12th. Day of People's Unity: November 4th.

INSURANCE Most European policies provide cover across all Russian territory west of the Urals. Many of the Western medical services have direct billing arrangements with major US insurance companies.

INTERNET Internet access is plentiful, with many cafés (McDonald's, TGI Fridays) offering free WiFi and others (Coffeemania, Koffee Haus, and Shokoladnitsa chains) making nominal charges. Cafe Max Internet cafés are open 24 hours, offering WiFi, broadband, and copying services. Their most central locations are at Nevsky Prospect d. 90–92 (☎ 812 273 6655, ☎ 812 272 6315) and within the Hermitage (☎ 812 710 9550). www.cafemax. ru. Alternatively, try Quo Vadis at Nevsky Prospect d. 76, ☎ 812 333 0708.

LOST PROPERTY Try the *Stol Nahodok* (literally the 'Lost Property Table') at Zakharyevskaya Ul. d. 19

☎ 812 578 3690, the lost property department at Moskovsky Vokzal (Nevsky Prospect d. 85 ☎ 812 768 4043), the Center for Lost Documents at Bolshaya Monetnaya Ul. d. 16 ☎ 812 336 5109, or the Lost Property desks at Pulkovo-1 (☎ 812 723 8361) and 2 (☎ 812 324 3787.

MAIL & POSTAGE   The main post office is at Pochtamtskaya d. 9 ☎ 812 312 3954: you'll need to visit this if sending parcels abroad. Most of the tourist hotels will sell you stamps: they're not readily available outside of post offices, however. Letters and postcards cost 22 rubles to any destination worldwide.

MINI HOTELS   Said to number more than 500. See p 147, or check member organizations of the St Petersburg Small Hotels Association at www.inspb.com.

MONEY   The ruble has been convertible since 2006, and some exchange bureaux (notably at Heathrow) hold rubles for exchange, although rates are dire. Exchanges are freely available throughout the city center, but you may be asked to show your passport at some. Be very careful if changing money at banks, especially any branch of Bank ВЕФК. Their advertised rates are good, but they will reject any notes they deem to be faulty, exchanging only at their 'protective' commission rate of 7%: and it's astonishing what they can find fault with. At press time, exchange rates were 1€=36.28R; 1$=25.07R; and 1£=44.55R. For up-to-the-minute currency rates check the currency converter website **www.xe.com/ucc**. Travelers checks can only be cashed in banks, and commission charges of 2%–3% are common. **Citibank** and **Raiffeisen Bank** have branches on Nevsky Prospect (Citibank at 45/2 ☎ 812 336 7575 and Raiffeisen at 102 ☎ 812 334

4343), with ATMs throughout the city (www.citibank.ru, www.raiffeisen.ru/en/). Commission charges at ATMs vary widely (and will depend on your own bank), but some can be punitive. If you plan to bring cash, euros are the currency of choice these days. **American Express** has an office at Malaya Morskaya Ul. d. 23 ☎ 812 326 45000. www.americanexpress.com/russia.

PASSPORTS   See 'Visas & Registration' on p 164. You are legally required to carry your passport at all times. Tourists can be fined if they cannot show their passport with registration stamps and documentation.

PHARMACIES   The **36.6** chain has branches throughout the city, several open 24 hours. Their most central location is at Nevsky Prospect d. 98 (☎ 812 275 8187), or call their Enquiry line, ☎ 812 275 8187.

PUBLIC TOILETS   Still woefully rare, although 'Superloos' (with running water and a 15–20 ruble charge) have started popping up in some areas. Chemical toilets are available throughout the city but should be avoided at all costs. Restaurants and bars are legally obliged to allow you to use their facilities: aim for one of the ubiquitous coffee chains—Coffee House, or Shokoladnitsa.

SAFETY   Visitors leaving certain clubs late at night may be at risk of assault and theft, and unlicensed cabs waiting for punters outside nightclubs can sometimes pose a threat. Generally though, tourists are undisturbed and women safe to walk the city center alone, even in the early hours.

SMOKING   A national sport. Non-smoking facilities are increasing, but still rare. Ask for *kuryashy* (Курящй: smoking) or *ne kuryashy* (не курящий: non-smoking).

TAXES   VAT is applied to most goods and services at a rate of 18%. It is included in all retail and restaurant bills, but check when paying for hotel accommodation.

TELEPHONES   If making long-distance calls outside St Petersburg from a landline, dial ☎ 8, wait for a tone, and then dial the local area code followed by the full number. For international calls, dial ☎ 8 and wait for a tone, then dial ☎ 10 before the country code. If dialling from a St Petersburg SIM mobile, simply dial ☎ 8 before the local area code.

TIPPING   Many wait staff are moonlighting students working for what are often criminally low wages, even here. Fifteen percent is about right, with 20 rubles or so for coat check staff.

TOURIST INFORMATION   There are **Tourist Information Centers** at Sadovaya Ul. d. 14/52 ☎ 812 310 2822 and at Dvortsovaya Pl. d. 12

☎ 982 8253. www.visit-petersburg. com. A **Tourist Information Line** is provided on ☎ 812 300 3333.

TRAVELERS WITH DISABILITIES   The Liberty Tour company specializes in travel for the disabled, offering tours of the Hermitage, the Peter Paul Fortress, the Russian Museum, and Peterhof, as well as special interest and general sightseeing tours. Their website (www.liberty tour.ru) includes a useful list of wheelchair-accessible hotels. The Moscow-based **Perspektiva** society works to promote disabled rights throughout Russia, and, again, is particularly helpful on wheelchair-accessible hotels. Contact them at 2nd Frunzenskaya Ul. d. 8, ☎ 495 245 6879, www.eng. perspektiva-inva.ru.

WATER   International media continue to report cases of *Giardia lamblia* (a particularly nasty intestinal parasite) among travelers foolhardy enough to drink the tap water. Locals will promise you the water these days is entirely safe: personal experience suggests you shouldn't believe them.

St Petersburg: **A Brief History**

9TH CENTURY The lands of the Neva become part of the Principality of Novgorod, a trading center with Europe and the Hanseatic League.

1700–1721 The Second Northern War. Peter I launches attack on what is now the Peter Paul Fortress.

1703 May 16th (27th Gregorian calendar): foundations are laid for the Peter Paul Fortress.

1713 St Petersburg becomes the capital city and rapid building occurs, including the Exchange,

the former Customs House, and the Summer Palace.

1723 University of St Petersburg founded.

1727 The first permanent bridge is built across the Neva.

1750S Petrine Baroque architecture takes hold (1750s) under Rastrelli and others, with the building of the Winter Palace, the Smolny Convent, Peterhof, and Tsarskoye Tselo. Neoclassical styles begin to dominate by the end of the 18th century, including the Kazan

Cathedral, St Isaac's Cathedral, the new Admiralty, the Senate, and the Mikhailovsky Palace.

1825 The Decembrist uprising, the first attempt to secure constitutional reforms, is put down and the leaders exiled.

1851 St Petersburg–Moscow railway opens. Industrial growth from the mid-19th century onwards increases the city's importance as a port.

1861 The emancipation of the serfs results in a more mobile labor force.

1881 Early revolutionaries the 'People's Will' movement assassinate Tsar Alexander II. Successor Alexander III initiates a period of repression and builds the Church of the Spilled Blood on the site.

1900 The population tops 1.5 million as the rural population moves to the new industrial factories. Poor infrastructure, utilities, and housing result in appalling conditions for the workers.

1905 Strikes begun in 1904, leading to the General Strike of 1905, culminating in the Bloody Sunday massacre on January 9th.

1914 Military fervor with the outbreak of WWI sees the city's name changed to the less Germanic 'Petrograd'.

1917 Population tops 2.5 million.

APRIL 1917 Lenin returns from exile.

1917 After failed attempts in July, troops storm the Winter Palace on October 25th as the Petrograd Soviet gains power over the Tsarist Provisional Government.

1918–1920 The Civil War decimates industry and agriculture, and the population drops to 722,000. The proximity of German troops persuades Lenin to move the capital to Moscow.

1924 The city is renamed 'Leningrad' following Lenin's death that year.

1928 The first Five Year Plan. Rapid industrial development sees the population hit 3,000,000 by 1939. Urban development of former working class areas sees the flourishing of Constructivist architecture, halted in 1935 when the new St Petersburg Plan results in the Stalinist architecture of new city development around Moskovsky Prospect.

1934 The assassination of popular party head Sergei Kirov in Smolny marks the start of the 'Great Terror'.

1941 Germans encircle the city and the 872-day Siege of Leningrad begins on September 8th. Two hundred thousand die in January and February 1942 alone.

JANUARY 1943 The Siege is partially breached when the Red Army defeats German forces to open a land corridor from Lake Ladoga.

27TH JANUARY 1944 The Siege is lifted as German forces retreat.

1948 Post-war redevelopment sees the city expand north and south. The St Petersburg metro opens in 1955.

1949–1950 The 'Leningrad Affair' sees 2,000 officials removed from their posts and six senior officials executed. Many are later exonerated under the Khrushchev Thaw.

1991 The country's first free elections on June 12th, see Perestroika reformist Anatoly Sobchak elected mayor and the city renamed St Petersburg. Sobchak protégé Vladimir Putin becomes head of external relations and begins a rapid rise to power.

2003 300th anniversary celebrations see the flourishing of new hotels and tourist facilities.

2006 St Petersburg's hosting of the G8 Summit is seen by many Russians as marking its return to the international stage.

Useful **Phrases & Menu Terms**

The Russian Alphabet

RUSSIAN	PRONUNCIATION
Аа	Ah
Бб	b (as in 'bus')
Вв	v (as in 'very')
Гг	g (as in 'go')
Дд	d (as in 'dog')
Ее	Yeh
Ёё	yö (as in 'yo-yo')
Зз	z (as in 'zoo')
Жж	zh (as in 'measure')
Ии	Ee (as in 'happy')
Йй	Ee (y as in 'yes')
Кк	K
Лл	l
Мм	m
Нн	n
Оо	o
Пп	p
Рр	r
Сс	S
Тт	T
Уу	U (pronounced as in 'zoo')
Фф	F
Хх	kh
Цц	ts
Чч	ch (as in 'check')
Шш	sh
Щщ	shch
Ъъ	Hard sign—always silent
Ыы	Y
Ьь	Soft sign—always silent
Ээ	eh
Юю	yu
Яя	ya

Useful Phrases

ENGLISH	RUSSIAN	PHONETIC
Hello	Здравствуйте!	Zdrastvuyte
Good morning	Доброе утро!	Dobroye utro
Good day	Добрый день!	Dobry den
Good evening	Добрый вечер!	Dobry vecher

ENGLISH	RUSSIAN	PHONETIC
Goodbye	До свидания!	Dosvidanya
Please	Пожалуйста	Pozhalusta
Thank you	Спасибо	Spasibo
Excuse me	Изините	Izvinite
Yes	Да	Da
No	Нет	Nyet
Good	Хорошо	Khorosho
Bad	Плохо	Plokho
I don't know	Я не знаю	Ya ne znayu
When?	Когда	Kagda?
Where?	Где	Gde?
Where is…?	Где находится….?	Gde nahoditsa?
How do I get to…?	Как дойти до…?	Kak doiti do?
On the left	Слева	Sleva
On the right	Справа	Sprava
Entrance	Вход	Vhod
Exit	Выход	Vihod
I would like…	Мне хотелось бы…	Mne hotelos bi
I need…	Мне нужно…	Mne nuszhno
Do you have…?	У Вас есть.?	Oo vas yest?
How much is…?	Сколько стоит	Skolko stoit?
Yesterday	Вчера	Vchera
Today	Сегодня	Sevodnya
Tomorrow	Завтра	Zavtra
More	Больше	Bolshe
Less	Меньше	Menshe
Do you speak English?	Вы говорите по-английски	Vy govorite po angliysky?
I don't understand	Я не понимаю	Ya ne ponimayu
What time is it?	Сколько сейчас времени?	Skolko sechas vremeni?
Do you have a menu in English?	У Вас есть меню на английском языке?	Oo vas yest menu na Angliskom yazike?
Could I have the bill please?	Можно счёт?	Mozhno schot?
Station	Вокзал	Vokzal
Stop (bus stop, metro etc.)	Остановка	Ostanovka
Metro	Метро	Metro
Airport	Аэропорт	Aeroport
Taxi	Такси	Taxi
Cathedral	Храм / Собор	Khram or Sobor
Church	Церковь	Tserkov
Museum	Музей	Moozei
Theater	Театр	Teatr
Restaurant	Ресторан	Restoran
Toilet	Туалет	Too-a-let
Male	Мужской	Muzhskoy
Female	Женский	Zhensky
I need a doctor	Мне нужен врач	Mne nuzhen vrach

ENGLISH	RUSSIAN	PHONETIC
I need to book a hotel room	Мне нужно забронировать комнату	Mne nuzhno zabronirovat komnatoo
I need to book a place	Мне нужно забронировать место	Mne nyzhno zabronirovat mesto
I need to book a ticket	Мне нужно забронировать билет	Mne nyzhno zabronirovat billet
I've lost my credit card	Я потерял свою кредитную карту (male); Я потеряла свою кредитную карту (female)	Ya poteryal svoyu kreditnooyoo kartoo (male); Ya poeteryala svoyu kreditnooyoo kartoo (female)
I've lost my passport	Я потерял (потеряла) свой паспорт	Ya poteryal (poteryala) svoy passport
I've lost my ticket	Я потерял (потеряла) свой билет	Ya poteryal (poteryala) svoy billet

Numbers

One	Один or Раз	Odin or Raz
Two	Два (masculine) Две (feminine)	Dva or Dve (feminine)
Three	Три	Tree
Four	Четыре	Chitiree
Five	Пять	Pyat
Six	Шесть	Shest
Seven	Семь	Seym
Eight	Восемь	Voseym
Nine	Девять	Devyat
Ten	Десять	Desyat
Twenty	Двадцать	Dvadtsat
Thirty	Тридцать	Tridtsat
Forty	Сорок	Sorok
Fifty	Пятьдесят	Pyatdesyat
Sixty	Шестьдесят	Shestdesyat
Seventy	Семьдесят	Semdesyat
Eighty	Восемьдесят	Vosemdesyat
Ninety	Девяносто	Devyanosto
One hundred	Сто	Sto
One thousand	(Одна) тысяча	Odna tisacha

Street Names & Abbreviations

Per.	pereulok or lane
Nab.	naberezhnaya or embankment
Ul.	ulitsa or street
d.	an abbreviation for 'dom' or house, used to show house numbers
M. or B.	if before a street name this is an abbreviation of Malaya (small) or Bolshaya (big) e.g., Malaya Lubyanka, Bolshaya Lubyanka are two different streets.
1st , 3rd, etc.	if used before a street name, this is an abbreviation of 1-aya, 2-aya meaning 'First Tverskaya-Yamskaya Ul.', for example.

Index

See also Accommodations and Restaurant indexes, below.

Photo **Credits**

Explore over 3,500 destinations.

TOKYO — 7766 miles
LONDON — 3818 miles
TORONTO — 4682 miles
SYDNEY — 5087 miles
NEW YORK — 4947 miles
LOS ANGELES — 2556 miles
HONG KONG — 5638 miles

Frommers.com makes it easy.

Find a destination. ✓ Book a trip. ✓ Get hot travel deals.
Buy a guidebook. ✓ Enter to win vacations. ✓ Listen to podcasts.
Check out the latest travel news. ✓ Share trip photos and memories.
And much more.

Frommers.com